The
Children's Book
of Knitting

The Children's Book of Knitting

JAN MESSENT

B.T. Batsford Limited,
London

First published 1990
© Jan Messent 1990

ISBN 0 7134 6330 9

Typeset by Tek-Art Ltd, Kent
Printed in Great Britain by
The Bath Press, Bath
for the publishers
B.T. Batsford Limited
4 Fitzhardinge Street
London W1H 0AH

Contents

Acknowledgement

Many of the 'how-to-do-it' drawings seen in this book were made especially by me for the Knitting Craft Group's teaching packs. The Director, Alec Dalglish, has kindly allowed me to use them so that I wouldn't have to draw them differently all over again! For saving me much arm-ache (and probably headache too) I thank Alec and gratefully acknowledge his co-operation.

Introduction

If you have ever watched someone knitting, you probably thought they 'just knew' how to do it without ever being, like you, a young beginner. Well, of course, the truth is that no one 'just knows' how to knit. Everyone has to be taught at some stage, and to learn while you are very young is the best time of all because young people don't mind making mistakes nearly as much as older people! And this is the most important thing about learning to knit – **not to mind making mistakes**. Someone famous once said, 'He who never made a mistake never made anything.' Way back in history, even very poor people who never learned to read or write could knit like fury: fine garments in richly-coloured yarns fit for kings and queens. The Peruvians of South America spin, dye *and* knit their own yarns to the most exciting designs while sitting outside their homes in the sun, and in Britain we see people sitting on park benches busily clicking away while the sparrows hop about their feet. It's an activity you can take anywhere – just tuck a piece of knitting into a bag or pocket and do a row or two in a spare moment; it's surprising how quickly it grows.

It's also surprising how easy it is to learn, so don't let anyone tell you that you're too young. Just pester them into letting you have a go. Look at the diagrams carefully and keep trying. Don't be afraid to ask for help, and when you have the hang of it, show someone else how to do it too! In no time at all you'll be a fully-fledged knitter, able to knit your own clothes and looking as if you always 'just knew' how to do it.

I do hope that this book gives you a lot of enjoyment and helps you to discover the pleasure that people all over the world find in knitting.

Jan Messent
April 1990

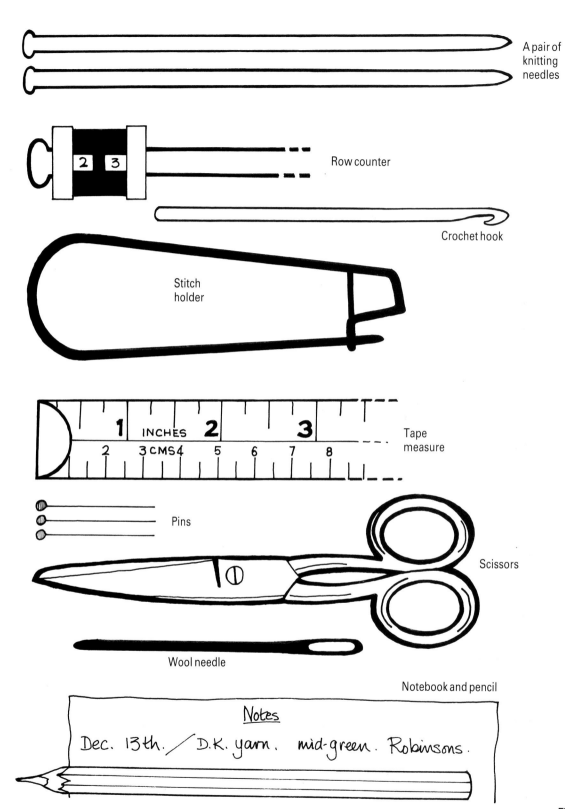

A pair of knitting needles

Row counter

Crochet hook

Stitch holder

Tape measure

Pins

Scissors

Wool needle

Notebook and pencil

Notes
Dec. 13th. / D.K. yarn. mid-green. Robinsons.

Fig 1

1

Tools

What shall I need?

Well, the simple answer is really very simple: just a pair of knitting needles and a ball of yarn. That's all. If that is what you have already, then you can begin to knit, but there are a few extras which would be quite useful, so here is a list of things which you could collect together as you go along, and keep them safely in a box or drawer so that they do not get lost or damaged.

- **Needles**, all sizes, but particularly sizes 4mm and 5mm which you will need for the patterns in this book.
- **A row-counter** is a little round plastic device which slides on to one of your needles. It has a dial which you alter after every row, and this will remind you how many rows you have knitted.
- **A crochet hook** (size 3.50mm) will be useful to help pick up stitches which accidently drop off the needle. (See page 00.)
- **A stitch holder** is rather like a huge safety pin. You can slide stitches on to this to keep them safe when you do not want to cast off.
- **A tape measure** is probably more useful to knitters than a ruler because it can measure round things as well as flat ones. You will certainly need one of these.
- **A pair of scissors** – another very important tool. Always cut yarn rather than trying to break it. Some yarn is so strong it is almost impossible to break it anyway! Keep them safe.
- **The wool needle** is not an ordinary sewing needle as it has a blunt point rather than a sharp one. It also has a very large eye for thick yarns to go through. Do not try to thread a needle with yarn in the same way that you do with sewing cotton, but fold the end of the yarn over the needle first and push the *fold* through the eye by nipping it with your finger and thumb. A wool needle is very large and thick and is sometimes called a 'tapestry needle'.
- **A pencil and notebook** are very useful for making notes of special things you need to remember: numbers of stitches, rows, which kind of yarn, where you bought it and how much it cost (and when) – all kinds of things. Always have one handy, and keep it specially for your knitting notes.
- **Pins**. The nicest ones to use are quite long, with round coloured ends so that they can easily be seen in the knitting. Keep them

Fig 2

safely in a box or on a pincushion when not in use. Always pin knitting so that the head of the pin is on the edge and the point towards the middle of the piece, that is, at a right-angle to the edge.

Which yarn, which needles?

Needles and yarns are made in different sizes and thicknesses so that our knitting can be as fine or as thick as we choose. As you become more used to knitting, you will learn to use all kinds of yarn, smooth, hairy and bumpy, wool, cotton and nylon and all kinds of mixtures. But for now, we will use the one known as **double knitting** (D.K. for short) because this is nice to handle, not too fine and not too thick. All the patterns in this book are made in D.K. yarn, except teddy's jacket and shorts.

As you become more proficient at knitting, you will also learn how to use different kinds of needles. The ones shown here are the kinds used mostly, but there are others too. They are not all the same length either, as you can see by the drawing (Fig 3). Many people like to use long needles because they find it comfortable to tuck the knob end under one arm (usually the right one) while they knit. This prevents the needle from wobbling about as they make the stitches. You might like to try doing this too, to see if it helps, but if you are only knitting a few stitches it is probably more comfortable to use medium length or short ones. Try to avoid using the coloured bendy plastic ones (often found in children's kits) as these are not very easy to knit with. Metal ones are better as they have good points.

When you are not using your knitting needles, keep them safely in a drawer or container away from small children. This way, they will always be clean, unscratched and safe. Scratched, bent and sticky needles are impossible to knit with, so never use your needles for anything other than your knitting.

The only size needles you will need for the patterns in this book are 4mm, and 5mm for the teddy bear's outfit, but it would be good fun to try out any others on some other knitting, just to see what they feel like. Don't forget to ask permission first, though!

A note on sizing

Some of the knitting needles you have at home may be quite old, and therefore will have a different set of numbers on them from more modern ones. This is because the system of sizing the needles has changed over the years. For example, if you find needles with a number 8 on them, this is the same as size 4mm and they will do just as well. How do you know which is an 'old' size and which is a 'new' size? Well, the new sizes all have the number followed by 'mm' (which means millimetre), and the old ones just have the number alone. If you can find a knitting needle gauge among the other tools, this will help you to make sure your needles are all the correct size.

The American sizing system is different again. The following table should help to make things clear.

'new' size	'old' size	US size
4mm	8	6
5mm	6	8

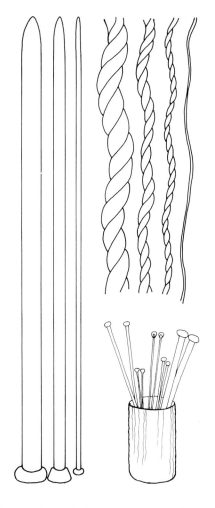

Fig 3

Tension (gauge)

Knitting patterns always tell us which kind of yarn and which size of needles to use together. This is because, if we used *any* yarn and *any* needles together, our knitting would be a different size and shape from the one in the pattern, and if we were making something to wear, this could be quite serious. So, to make sure that everyone gets it right, the pattern tells us how many stitches and rows should fit inside an exact measurement, and they call the result the **tension** (or **gauge**). The idea is that we should check to see that our tension is the same as the one in the pattern because some people knit tighter or looser than others.

Fig 4

Too loose?
Use finer needles

Too tight?
Use thicker needles

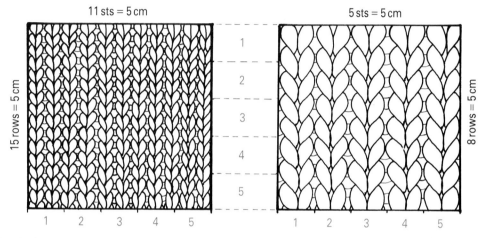

11 sts = 5 cm

15 rows = 5 cm

5 sts = 5 cm

8 rows = 5 cm

Fig 5 Tension

This is written in the pattern as:

11 sts and 15 rows = 5 cm
on size 4 mm needles.

This is written in the pattern as:

5 sts and 8 rows = 5 cm
on size 6½ mm needles.

The easiest way to do this is to make a piece of knitting using the same yarn and needle size as those in the pattern. A 10cm (4 inch) square would be about right. Then take a white postcard and measure a 5cm (2 inch) square (very exactly) in the middle, and cut this out to make a window. Place this window over your knitted piece and pin it down. Now count the number of stitches (across) and the number of rows (down) which can be seen inside the window. Write this down on a piece of paper.

You may find that there are quite a lot of stitches and rows inside the window, like the drawing on the left in Fig 5, or not very many, like the one on the right. This is because the one on the right has been made with thicker yarn and needles than the other one.

Now check your result against the tension given in the pattern. Too many stitches and rows means that you should use slightly thicker needles. This will make your stitches a little bigger so that fewer of them will fit into the square, like larger apples in a small box!

Too few stitches means that you should use slightly finer needles so that your stitches close up together more. This is like people squeezing up closer together on a seat to make more room for someone else!

Too many rows to fit the square window? Then just knit a few less. Not enough rows to fit? Knit a row or two more, but always be sure to write down any changes you make, such as needle size, number of stitches or rows, in your notebook.

How much yarn shall I need?

Knitting patterns also tell us how much yarn we shall need to make the article or garment. The trouble is that some patterns (like those in this book) tell you that you will need double knitting yarn even when they know that not all double knitting yarn is exactly the same thickness. Well, the good news for you is that none of the patterns in this book is for people to wear, only for toys, and they don't seem to mind wearing our first attempts! So it will not matter too much if some of the yarns you use are just a little thicker than others, even though they are all called double knitting. If there is obviously going to be a big difference, you can always adjust the number of stitches you cast on by adding or subtracting one or two. If you have to change yarns in the middle of a piece (as when you need to change colour) and find that one yarn is much thicker than the other, just do an increase or decrease in the middle of the row — that should do the trick, and is actually how I managed to keep my knitting straight on these small projects.

What does a ball of yarn weigh?

We buy balls of yarn weighing 20gms, 25gms, 50gms, 100gms and sometimes more, but we often have oddments at home which have been partly used, and have lost their labels, and we have no way of knowing whether we have enough or not. Remember the kitchen scales where flour, sugar and butter are weighed? Well, they will weigh your yarn in grams or ounces too: just put

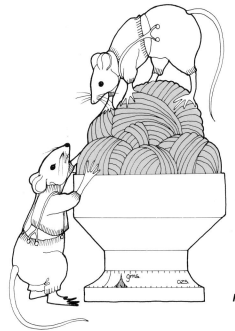

Fig 6

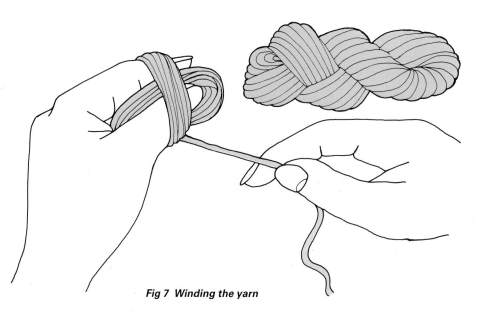

Fig 7 Winding the yarn

your yarn in the clean weighing-pan and see what the pointer says.

By the way, don't throw away the paper band which goes round a new ball of yarn. This is called the **ball band** and tells you what the yarn is called, who made it, how much it weighs, what it is made of, how it should be washed, which needles to use, and all kinds of other useful things. When you take it off, roll it up into a little sausage and tuck it down into the middle of the ball for safe keeping.

How to wind yarn

Sometimes we buy yarn in skeins, or hanks, that is, in a coil which is then twisted upon itself, and we have to wind it into balls before we can use it. At one time, all yarn was bought like this, but nowadays we can buy it ready-wound.

To wind from a hank, it must be carefully loosened from its coil and then held between someone's outstretched hands while it is wound. The important thing to remember is, that while holding the yarn in one hand, the wrapping is done over the tops of the fingers and thumb too, as shown in the drawing. After a few wraps, remove the fingers gently, turn the bundle over, and wrap again in the same way in the other direction. This is to allow the yarn to relax again after it has been stretched during winding (Fig 7).

What the pattern means

In knitting, there are two ways of using the word **pattern**. The way it is used in the heading (above) refers to the written instructions for a complete article, whether a garment or a mug-muff, and these simply tell you what you must do from start to finish. This is called a **knitting pattern**.

But you may also see the words **stitch pattern**, and this refers to the stitches used to make a pattern *on the knitting*, such as moss stitch, garter stitch or double rib. It might also mean a pattern of colours like the star pattern on Santa's sack, but this has nothing to do with the *shape* of the piece you are knitting.

Knit is another word which may be used in two different ways, either to mean 'make a piece of fabric by knitting', or 'use the knit stitch instead of the purl stitch'. To avoid getting mixed up, the patterns in this book have sometimes used the word **work** instead, as in

cast on 20 sts and work in stocking stitch . . .

because, as you will see later on, stocking stitch

is made by knitting *and* purling, and if the pattern had said, 'knit in stocking stitch . . .' you might understandably be a little puzzled about exactly what is meant. So when the patterns in this book tell you to knit, they mean you to *use the knit stitch* until you are told to change.

Abbreviations

In knitting patterns, some words have to be used over and over again, for example, 'stitches, knit two together, increase and decrease'. These words take up a lot of room on a page and if they were to be written out in full every time, the pattern would use up reams of paper and so cost more. So people who write these patterns use a shortened form of the most often-used words, and these are called **abbreviations**. It's really a kind of shorthand. Fortunately, most patterns use the same abbreviations, so once you have learnt their meanings, you will be able to read any knitting pattern, and only have to learn a few more every now and again.

The following list is not a complete one, but tells you the meaning of the ones used in this book.

st(s)	–	stitch(es)
k	–	knit
p	–	purl
dec	–	decrease
inc	–	increase
k2tog	–	knit two stitches together
D.K.	–	double knitting yarn
g.st	–	garter stitch
ss	–	stocking stitch
ins	–	inches
cm	–	centimetres
mm	–	millimetres
gms	–	grams
R.S.	–	right side (either the right-hand side, or the right side of the work)
W.S.	–	wrong side
L.S.	–	left side

these are more general abbreviations which you may already know

i.e.	–	that is
e.g.	–	for example

Brackets A

Another way of saving space in a knitting pattern is used when the instructions for a row are made up of repeated 'movements'. Supposing, for instance, you were told to:

Row 7: k2, k2tog, k2, k2tog, k2, k2tog, k2, k2tog, k2

This takes up quite a lot of space and it is also difficult for you to see where you are without getting lost somewhere along the line. So instructions like this can be shortened by placing the 'movement' inside brackets, followed by a number which tells you how many times to repeat them. Anything left **outside the brackets** means that this should be worked once, but *not* repeated. So the abbreviation for the movement above would be

Row 7: (k2, k2tog) 4 times, k2

Or it might be written like this instead:

Row 7: k2, (k2tog, k2) 4 times

Either way is exactly the same, so don't forget to read the whole line.

Brackets B

Sometimes it helps you to know how many stitches there are supposed to be at the end of an increase or decrease row, just to check that you're on the right lines. So here and there you will find a number inside brackets at the end of a row, like this (38 sts). Count your stitches to see if you have the same number.

Measurements

Lengths and widths have been given in both inches and centimetres so that anyone reading these patterns can choose which to use. But to make things a little simpler for readers, the two measurements are only more-or-less the same, not exactly.

More help with knitting

There are many books about knitting which will explain other things you may need to know as you progress, like cabling (twisted knitting), different shaping methods and fancy stitches. Look out for these in libraries and bookshops.

Watch closely to see how other people knit, how they hold the needles and yarn, and how fast they can reach the end of the row. Some people can actually read a book at the same time! Try out different ways of holding *your* needles and yarn to see how it feels. Ask people to show you in *slow motion* how they knit. Learn what you can about the history of knitting. The section which follows may show you how interesting this can be. What else can you discover?

Knitting gossip

The oldest piece of knitted fabric was found in a region of Arabia.

The Anglo Saxons did not knit.

In 1615, a black ewe was stolen in Shetland and the thief used its fleece to make a pair of socks.

At one time, socks and stockings were made by all members of the family in many rural parts of the country. Often a woman would card, spin *and* knit the wool, and then sell a pair of socks, for eight pence a pair in 1799. She might make as many as four pairs a week if she worked very hard.

Many soldiers and sailors knitted, including some very famous ones. Also priests, bishops, surgeons, builders, musicians, artists, actors, sportsmen – and my dentist!

Wives of fishermen have traditionally knitted waterproof jerseys to keep out the cold and wet during work. The patterns vary, depending on the region. We know them now as 'Fisherman Knits', Arans and Ganseys.

About one hundred years ago, a coarse and undyed yarn was used for some articles, such as caps and socks, knitted on thick needles. It was known as *bump*.

A certain William Lee invented a knitting frame in the late 1500s to take the place of hand knitting. At that time, no one was interested because they feared that the work of hand knitters would no longer be needed, preventing them from earning the money which they so badly needed.

There are several portraits of the Virgin Mary knitting, painted in Italy in the fourteenth century.

In Tudor times, only the men knitted.

In America, stocking stitch is called 'stockinette' and cast off is called 'bind off'.

The people of the Shetland Isles are famous for their very fine lace knitting. For this, they use a very fine yarn from the local sheep which they call 'Cobweb'.

Many years ago, people would knit while looking after their sheep, or walking to market. Nowadays, people knit on train, car and air journeys, and on buses, on the tube and at stations. They also knit at the dentist and in hospital waiting rooms to keep their minds busy.

You can see many knitting articles of great age in the museum at Hawes in North Yorkshire.

In sixteenth-century England, gentlemen courtiers wore very fine knitted stockings of silk. Often they would have the pattern of a clock worked into the side of the leg, just above the ankle, and this can be seen in some old portraits.

King Charles I wore a fine knitted shirt at his execution on 31 January 1649. This can still be seen in the London Museum, near the Barbican.

The first knitting needles were made of fine wire, sometimes of bone, wood and bamboo.

There are dozens of ways of casting on and off. See how many you can discover from those people whom you know can knit.

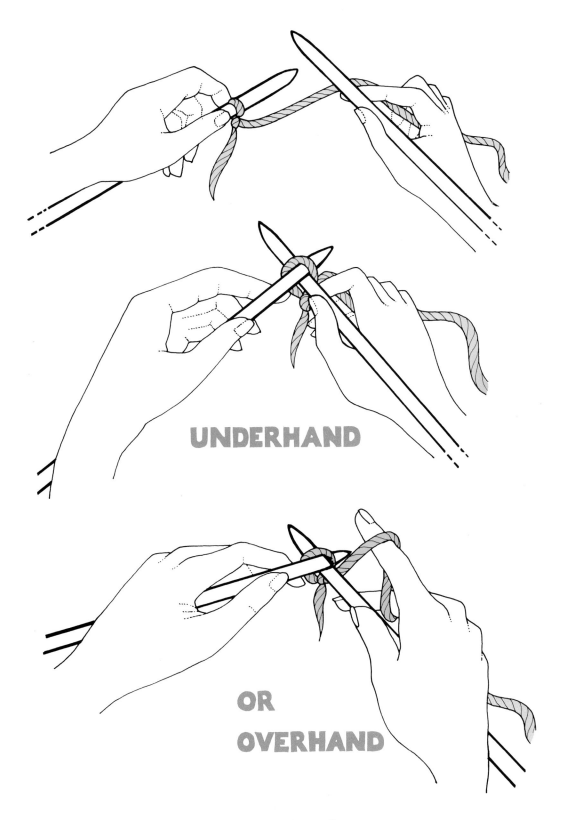

UNDERHAND

OR

OVERHAND

Fig 8 Holding the needles

Beginning to Knit

The slip knot (Fig 9)

The first stitch on the needle has to be tied on in a special way. It is called a **slip knot** or **slip stitch**, and the pictures (Fig 9) show how it is made.

1. Cross the yarn over itself to make a loop.
2. Take the long end and pass it behind the loop. Hold this in your left hand.
3. Take a knitting needle and, from the front, pick this yarn up with the point.
4. Pull the yarn up gently through the loop, holding the 'tail end' in your left hand.
5. Keep hold of the 'tail' and pull it to tighten the knot, then pull the other end of the yarn to make the loop fit snugly on to the needle.

This is your first stitch, and all other stitches are made from this one.

Holding the needles (Fig 8)

To put more stitches on to the same needle, you need the other one of the pair to help you, one needle in each hand. You can hold them in any way which feels most comfortable: every-one has their own special way of knitting and all of these work perfectly well, but here are two ways for you to try out. One is the **underhand method**, which is how you hold your pencil to write, and the other is the **overhand method**, which is how you hold a knife when you are cutting.

The slip stitch, which you have just made, is on the needle in your left hand. The empty needle and the **supply yarn** (which is the yarn coming from the ball which you will make stitches with)

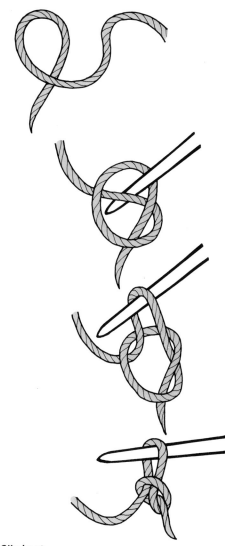

Fig 9 Slip knot

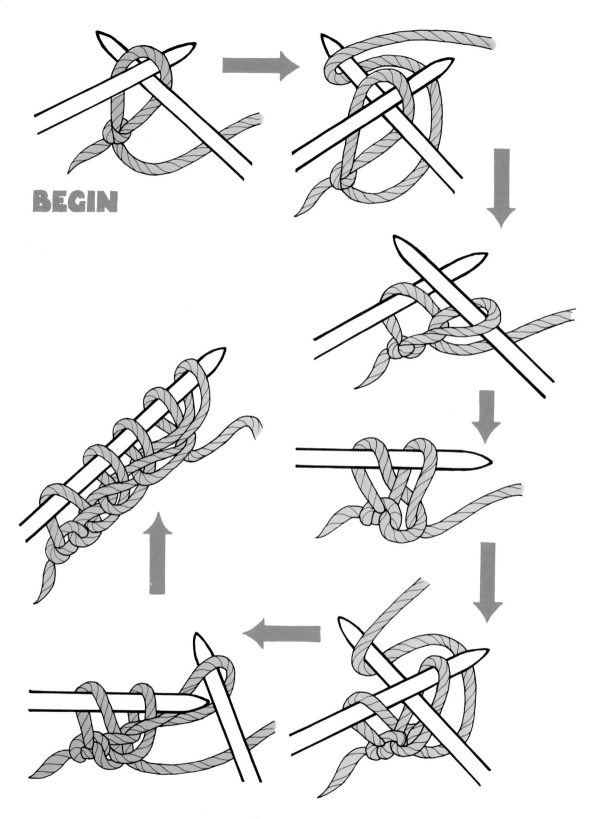

BEGIN

Fig 10 Casting on

are in your right hand. Try to keep the yarn in your right hand *all the time* instead of dropping it, as you will need it every time you make a new stitch. You can do this by winding it around the little finger of your right hand, but don't get too worried about this while you are learning to make stitches.

See how the right hand (R.H.) needle is pushed into the stitch on the left hand (L.H.) needle. Try this for yourself and then check with the picture (Fig 10, opposite) to see if you are correct.

Casting on – making the first set of stitches

Fig 10 shows how easy this is: just follow the arrows round the page in a clockwise direction.

1. Begin: R.H. needle into the slip knot.
2. Take the supply yarn in the R.H. and wrap it over the point of the R.H. needle.

Hold the yarn and the R.H. needle both together quite firmly.
3. Use the point of the R.H. needle to pull the yarn through the slip knot.
   This makes a new loop – a stitch!
4. Now use the point of the L.H. needle to take this new loop and put it next to the slip stitch, side by side.
   Now there are two stitches.
5. The R.H. needle will now be empty again. To make more stitches, put the empty (R.H.) needle between the two stitches on the L.H. needle, wrap the yarn over again, pull through, and let the L.H. needle pick up the new stitch to make a third, alongside the others.
6. Keep on doing this until you have as many stitches as you need on your L.H. needle.

Easy isn't it? Now you are ready to knit.

The knit stitch (Fig 11)

Now you have some stitches, you can begin to knit. Follow the arrows around the drawing and say to yourself '**in, over, through, off**'. That's really all there is to it.

Put the needle with the stitches on it in your L.H. and the empty needle in your R.H. Take the supply yarn in your R.H. too. Let's begin:

In. Needle into the first stitch. Look at the picture to check that it is in the right place.

Over. Yarn over the point of the R.H. needle. Pull it to the back out of the way, and hold it again in your R.H.

Through. Use the point of the R.H. needle to pull the yarn through the loop. Keep this new loop on the R.H. needle, and –

Off. Slip the 'old' stitch (which you have just knitted into) off the L.H. needle.

This makes one *less* on the L.H. needle and one *more* on the R.H. needle.

Fig 11 The knit stitch (RH)

Next stitch: '**in, over, through, off**'.
Then the next one: 'in, over, through, off; in, over, through . . . .'

If you keep on like this, all the stitches will move to the R.H. needle, and the L.H. needle will be empty. You will have knitted one whole row. Count your stitches again, just to check they are all still there.

To make the next row

One row completed. Now for the next one. Change over needles: put the full needle back into the L.H. and the empty one in the R.H.

Begin: 'in, over, through, off' into the first stitch. Keep the supply yarn always at the back of the needles, out of the way. If you let it get in front, you may find that you have made an extra stitch without wanting to. At the end of each row, check your stitches to see that extra ones have not crept on accidently.

As you make each new row, your knitting will grow and you will soon need to count the rows as well as the stitches.

Counting the rows (garter stitch) (Fig 12)

Garter stitch is the name we use when *every row* is knitted. To count the rows, this is what you do:

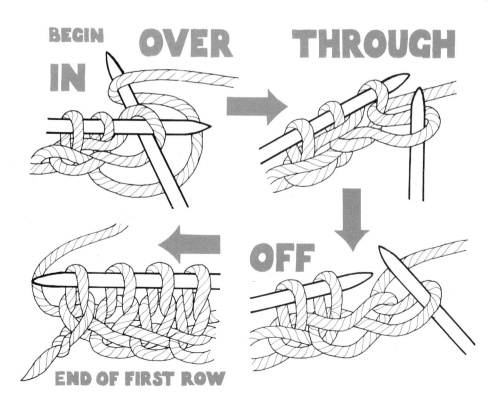

BEGIN IN OVER THROUGH OFF END OF FIRST ROW

1. Place the piece of knitting flat in front of you with its **starting tail** on the *left*, as it is in the drawing. If the needle now points towards the *right*, ready to work the next row, you will have worked an *even* number of rows. If the needle points to the *left*, you will have worked an *odd* number of rows.

2. Look carefully at the lower edge of Fig 12 and you will see what looks like a cord (or rope) with a row of 'vee' shapes stuck into it. This is the **cast-on edge** (cord and vee together) and is *not counted* when you begin to count the rows above.

3. The first knitted row begins where you see the lower arrow, that is, on the second row of vee shapes. On the other side of the knitting, these vees will be bumps, and the bumps will be vees. They are tucked partly underneath the first row of bumps. Every vee row will be an *odd number*.

4. The second knitted row is the lowest row of bumps seen on this side, and this means that every row of bumps on this side will be an *even number* (upper arrow).

5. All the *odd* rows are *vees* which lie between the bump rows. Now begin to count from the first vee row, bumps then vees, then bumps, and so on, upwards until you reach the needle.

There are eight rows on this piece of knitting.

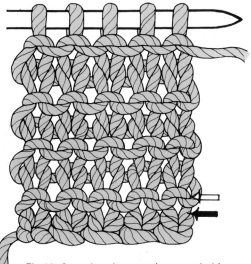

Fig 12 Counting the rows (garter stitch)

The knit and purl stitches for left-handed people

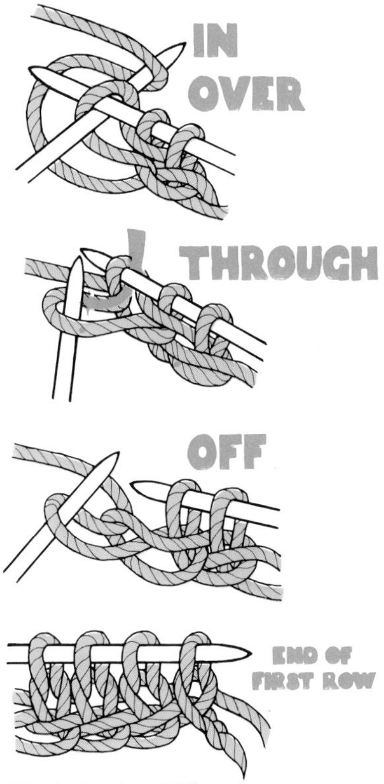

IN OVER

THROUGH

OFF

END OF FIRST ROW

Fig 13 The knit stitch (LH)

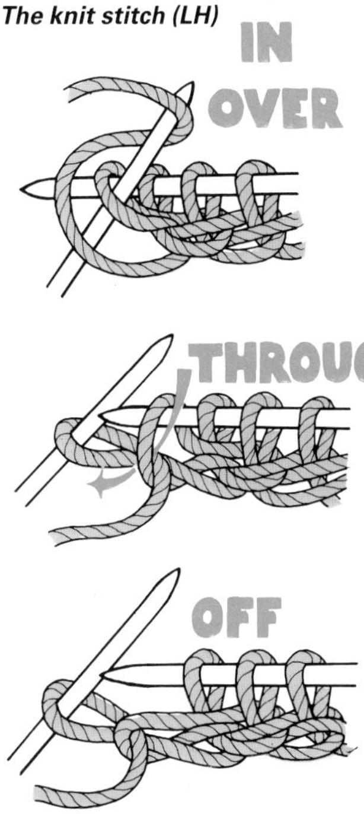

IN OVER

THROUGH

OFF

Fig 14 The purl stitch (LH)

The purl stitch (Fig 15)

The purl stitch is not much different from the knit stitch; it is simply made from the other side, that's all. The most important thing to remember about both stitches, is that in the **knit** stitch, the yarn is carried *behind* the needles; in the **purl** stitch, the yarn is carried *in front of* the needles.

Keep this rule in your head while you are knitting, because if the yarn is allowed to stray on to the wrong side, extra stitches which you do not want will appear.

Look at the pictures on this page and notice how the R.H. needle is put into the *front* of the stitch on the L.H. needle, and how the yarn is wrapped over from the *front*, instead of from the back.

Make the stitch 'in, over, through, off' as before, making each new stitch on the R.H. needle and allowing the 'old' one to drop off the L.H. needle.

Making both knit and purl stitches allows you to choose which side of your knitting to drop the loops of the old stitch. If you notice the way these loops drop (the 'off' stage) when you knit, you will see that they land on the side furthest away from you. When you purl, these loops stay on the side nearest to you.

Stocking stitch (Fig 16)

If you choose, you can make all the loops drop off on to the same side of your knitting, making the other side smooth. We do this by making one row of knit stitches followed by one row of purl stitches. This is called 'stocking stitch' because it is thought that this was used to make the fine hand-knitted stockings worn in the seventeenth century by courtiers at the Elizabethan and Stuart courts.

Fig 16 shows what stocking stitch looks like on both sides. The left-hand picture shows how the knitting looks when the knit row has just been made and the stitches are all on the R.H. needle.

Now turn the knitting round and put the full needle into your left hand ready to begin a new row. The right-hand picture (Fig 16) shows how this will look. The bumpy side is now facing you, and this is how you know that the purl row comes next.

When you have made the purl row, turn the knitting round again ready to begin the next row: full needle in the left hand, empty needle in the right hand. You will then have the smooth side facing you and this will remind you that the next row is a knit row.

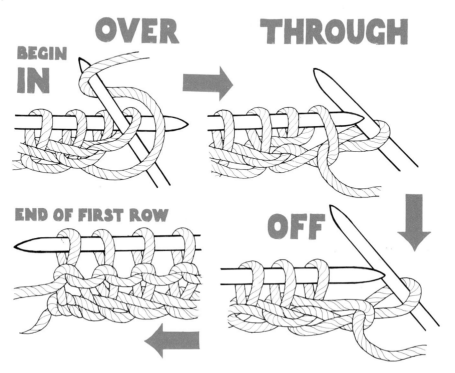

Fig 15 The purl stitch (RH)

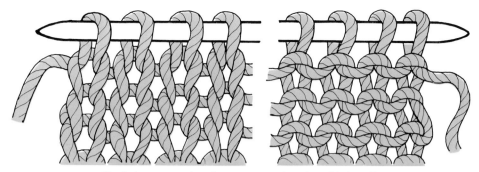

The knit row completed; turn over to the other side (needle in left hand) and begin the purl row

Fig 16 Stocking stitch

The other side of the smooth stocking stitch is just as useful. It is known as **reverse stocking stitch** and we sometimes use this as the right side instead of the other.

Counting the rows (stocking stitch)

1. Place the piece of knitting flat in front of you with its **starting tail** on the *left*. If the needle now points towards the *right* (ready to work the next row) you will have worked an *even* number of rows. If the needle points to the *left*, you will have worked an *odd* number of rows. This rule is just the same as for garter stitch. However, with stocking stitch, you can easily tell, because if you *began* with a knit row, all knit rows will be odd ones and all purl rows will be even ones.

2. As with garter stitch, do not count the cast-on edge into your rows. The cast-on edge is the very bottom (cord-like) edge with a row of vees tucked into it. The first knitted row begins where you see the second row of vees.

3. In stocking stitch, all the vee rows are on one side and the bump rows are on the reverse side. This makes it much easier to count, as all stitches on the R.S. are vees which stack up one above the other. These are what you count, moving upwards towards the needle. Use the point of your other knitting needle and poke it into the centre of each vee as you count: you will soon learn to do this quite easily without getting lost.

4. **Important**: the *last* row to be counted is not the one below your needle, but the *actual stitches on the needle*. This was the last row just purled, and in the drawing (Fig 17) is row 6.

Note: you will see by the way that the vees lead up to the stitches on the needle that it is the right-way-up vees that you should look for rather than the upside-down vees, which are really two half-stitches side by side.

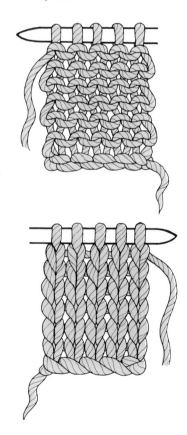

| **Remember** | smooth side | = | knit |
| | rough side | = | purl |

Fig 17 Counting the rows (stocking stitch)

Casting off

To **cast off** means to remove some stitches from the needle either at the end of a piece of knitting or to make a shape. You can cast off anywhere along the row, at the beginning only, in the middle, or from beginning to the end.

To cast off (knitwise) the stitches first have to be knitted two at a time. So to begin, knit two stitches in the usual way. Now use the point of the L.H. needle to lift the first one from the R.H. needle up and over the top of the second one. The two drawings show how this is done. Then let the stitch drop off the needle, as seen in the third picture.

Now you only have one stitch left on the R.H. needle. Knit another one, and lift the 'old' one over the 'new' one again.

Keep on doing this but *count how many lift-overs you do*, as this is the number of stitches you will have cast off. You will always finish with one stitch on the R.H. needle, so when you reach the end of the row, you must pull this last stitch up very loosely to make a large loop. Now cut the yarn and pass the end of it through this loop and pull firmly to make the knot sit snugly against the knitting.

Shaping

To cast off a few stitches at the beginning of a row, count how many lift-overs you have done as these are cast-off stitches. The one left on the R.H. needle is counted as one of the others left over, and you can then continue to knit on to the end of the row.

To shape in the same way on the other edge of the knitting, cast off at the beginning of the *next row* when this edge is nearest the point of the needle.

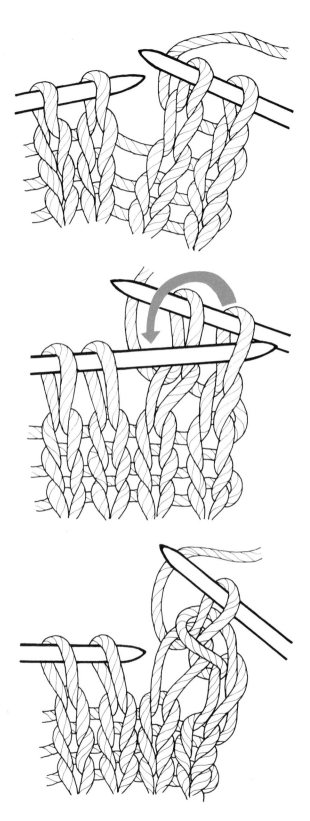

Fig 18 Casting off knitwise

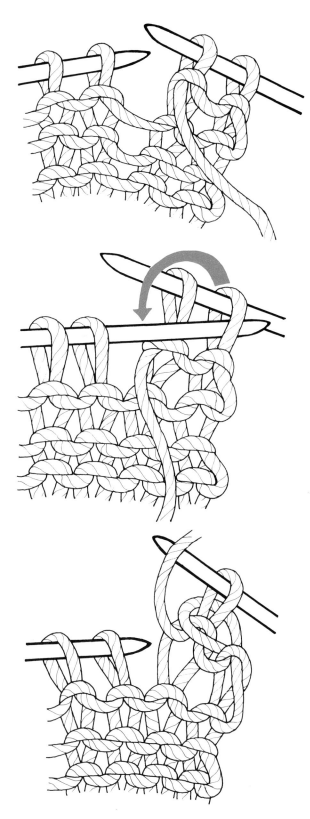

Cast off purlwise

This is done in exactly the same way as cast off knitwise, except that you must use the purl stitch instead of the knit stitch. Keep the yarn at the front and out of the way while you lift one stitch over the other.

Cast off in pattern

Sometimes the pattern instructions tell us to 'cast off in pattern'. This simply means that if you have been using both knit *and* purl stitches on the same row (for instance, in ribbing or moss stitch) you should also cast off using *both* knit and purl stitches where you would normally be using them on that row. Remember, when you do this, to bring the yarn over to the front before you purl a stitch and keep it there while you lift over. Then take it to the back again to make the knit stitch and keep it there until you have made the lift-over.

Fig 19 Casting off purlwise

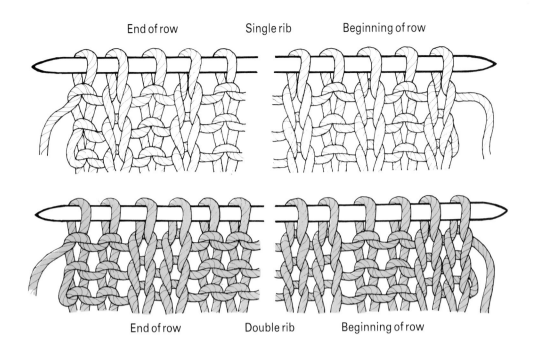

End of row   Single rib   Beginning of row

End of row   Double rib   Beginning of row

Fig 20   Single rib and double rib

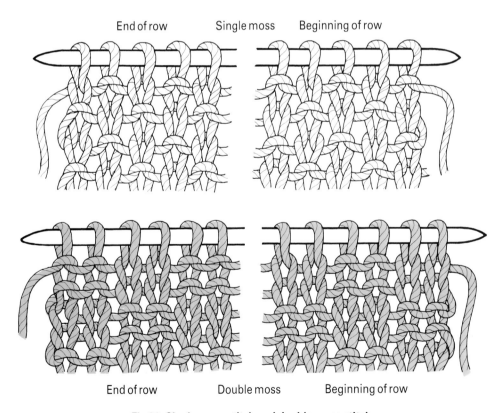

End of row   Single moss   Beginning of row

End of row   Double moss   Beginning of row

Fig 21   Single moss stitch and double moss stitch

CHAPTER 3

Now I Can Knit

Using knit and purl stitches together

Now that you understand how to knit and purl, there are many patterns for you to try, all of them using *both* stitches in the same row.

Reminder

To knit, hold the yarn at the back of the needles.

To purl, hold the yarn in front of the needles.

When you change from knit to purl, bring the yarn forward.

When you change from purl to knit, take the yarn behind again.

Single rib

You will need an *even* number of stitches on your needle (only part of a row is shown in the drawing) as this pattern is worked in pairs of stitches. *Check the list of abbreviations.*

Row 1: k1, p1. Continue like this to the end of the row. Turn.

Row 2: k1, p1, to the end of the row.

Every row is the same, beginning with a knit stitch and ending with a purl stitch.

Double rib

This stitch pattern is worked in groups of four, so you must be able to divide the number of stitches on your needle by four. (Did you realise that you would need to know some arithmetic?) Every row is worked k2, p2, k2, p2, to the end of the row.

Ribbing is often used for cuffs and welts of jumpers to keep them closer to the body than the other parts. You will see how much narrower the knitting becomes when ribs are used compared to garter stitch and stocking stitch, even with the same number of stitches.

Other rib patterns can be made by a k3, p3, arrangement, or even other variations like k2, p1, and k6, p3. Of course, with these patterns, not every row will be the same, only alternate ones.

Single moss stitch

This is a pretty pattern made in the same way as single rib, except that, because it is worked on an *odd* number of stitches, the vees and bumps do not stack above each other in rows. Look at Fig 21 to see what happens. Cast on an odd number of stitches and work every row k1, p1, to the end, but *always begin with a knit stitch*.

Double moss stitch

This is similar to single moss stitch except that the stitches are worked in pairs, so you need a number of stitches which can be divided by four (just as you do for double rib). On this pattern, you will have to be more aware of which row you are working, so you may find a row-counter useful. The first stitch changes every two rows, like this:

Rows 1 and 2: k2, p2, to the end of the row.

Rows 3 and 4: p2, k2, to the end of the row.

Then change back to rows 1 and 2 again, and repeat the 4 rows.

Increase and decrease

There are all kinds of reasons why we might need to alter the number of stitches on our needles,

Double moss st

Moss st

Single rib

Double rib

Reverse
stocking st

Stocking st

Garter st

Fig 22

either to make more, or to make less. There are
several ways of doing so, but only one is shown in
each case.

To increase (to make more stitches on the needle)

To increase, we have to make two stitches out of
one, and this is done by knitting twice into the
same stitch, once into the front (as usual) and then
again into the back. In the first drawing below, you
take the stitch 'in, over, through', but *don't* slide
the old one off. Instead, take the point of the R.H.
needle again into the *back* of the loop (see where
the arrow is pointing) and make another 'in, over,
through, off', as in the second drawing. Now you
should have two stitches where there was one
before.

This can be done anywhere along the row,
either at the beginning (as the drawing shows), in
the middle or at the end – or all three places! This
method is called 'increase into back of stitch', and
sometimes just 'increase' (or 'inc.').

To decrease (to make fewer stitches on the needle)

There are also several different ways of getting rid
of some stitches, but simply dropping a stitch off
the needle won't do, as this would make a ladder!
Instead, we will use the simplest method: knitting
two stitches together at the same time. The
drawings (Fig 24) show how this is done at the
end of a row, but it can be done anywhere you
wish.

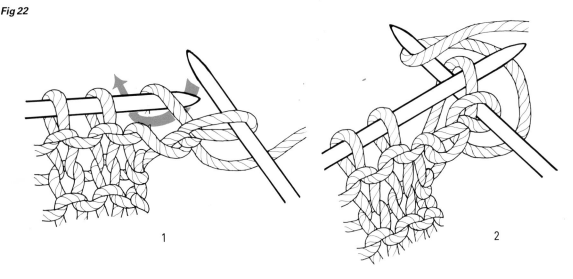

1   2

Fig 23 To increase

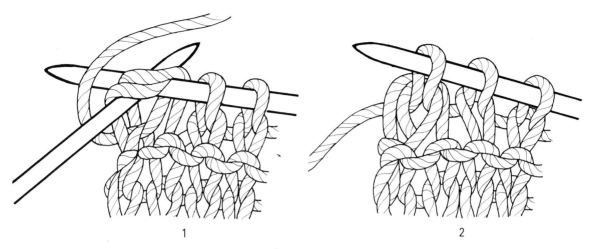

Fig 24 To decrease

In the first drawing above, put the R.H. needle 'in' into two stitches together, then 'over, through, off' as you see in the second drawing. Now there is only one stitch where there were two before. This method is called 'knit two together' (or 'k2tog').

An experiment in shaping

Shaping is just a simple matter of knowing how to cast on, cast off, increase and decrease: if you can do these things, then shaping is no problem! You can make shapes in garter stitch (all knitting) or in stocking stitch (one row knit, one row purl) but remember that the results will depend on which stitch you use. All stitches do not produce the same shape.

Look below at the two drawings of triangles. The garter stitch sample has produced a shorter triangle with a right-angle at the top; the stocking stitch sample is taller. But they both had exactly the same number of stitches and rows, and were knitted on the same yarn and needles. You can try this out for yourself, and use the triangles as roofs for cottages on a knitted panel.

Garter stitch triangle

Cast on 14 sts and knit 2 rows.
Row 3: (fasten a safety-pin to this side to remind you that you must decrease at *both ends* of this row every time the safety-pin is nearest you.) Now knit 2 stitches together (k2tog), k10, and then knit the last 2 stitches together. Now there are 12 sts on the needle.

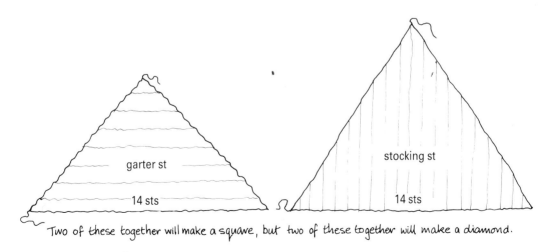

garter st

14 sts

stocking st

14 sts

Two of these together will make a square, but two of these together will make a diamond.

Fig 25 Shaping

Row 4: knit
Row 5: (safety-pin on your side) k2tog, k8, k2tog (10 sts)
Row 6: knit
Keep on decreasing (k2tog) at each end of *every other* (called alternate) row, until you have only 2 sts left. Lift the first of these (that means the one you knitted first) over the top of the other (like casting off). Cut the yarn and pass the end through the loop and pull gently. Now your triangle should look like the one in the drawing.

Stocking stitch triangle

Cast on 14 sts
Row 1: knit
Row 2: purl
Row 3: k2tog, k10, k2tog
Row 4: purl
Row 5: you will have seen now that your decreases (k2tog) at each end of the row only happen on knit rows. Continue as for the garter stitch triangle, decreasing on every alternate row, which has a purl row between.

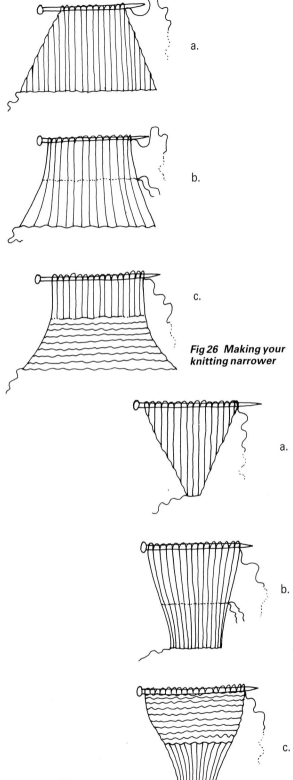

a.

b.

c.

Fig 26 Making your knitting narrower

a.

b.

c.

Fig 27 Making your knitting wider

A shaping reminder list

To make your knitting narrower:
● make fewer stitches on the needle by decreasing
● change to finer needles and yarn
● change the stitch pattern, for example, to ribbing

To make your knitting wider:
● make more stitches on the needle by increasing
● change to thicker needles and yarn
● change the stitch pattern, for example, to garter stitch

More shapes – no increases or decreases!

To make a tube (Fig 28)

Knit a rectangle (a), then sew the two sides together (b). Now you have a tube (c) which is how sleeves are made. It could also be the stalk of a toadstool, the trunk of a tree, or the body/sleeves of a teddy's jumper.

To make a humbug cushion (Fig 29)

Knit two squares (a). Sew them together on three sides only (b) from the W.S. Turn to the R.S. and pad the inside firmly, then fold the top across in the opposite direction (c) and sew up from the

R.S. Make it in black and white stripes like a humbug, or in many colours. Sew pompons or tassels to each corner.

To make a circle (Fig 30)

Knit a long narrow rectangle (a) in any stitch, then sew the two short sides together (b) to make a tube. Gather all round the top edge with a running stitch (c) leaving the beginning of the gathering thread loose. Draw the thread up and tie the two ends together tightly. Even the gathers all round (d) and you will have a circle which could become a biscuit, a wheel, a hat, the top of a toadstool or the base of a basket. (Fill it with pompon flowers like the flower-seller on page 44.)

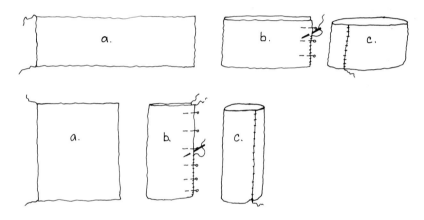

Fig 28 To make a tube

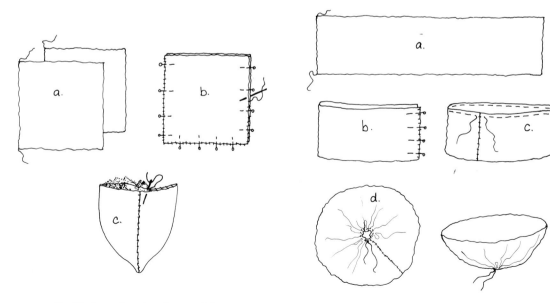

Fig 29 To make a humbug cushion

Fig 30 To make a circle

Knitting in two colours/changing yarns

Changing colours is a simple matter of changing yarns. Let us begin by making stripes in two colours. Use two colours of the same type of D.K. yarn, if possible. Each stripe is two rows tall, just there and back.

The method is the same whether you are working in garter stitch or stocking stitch, but you should always begin the new yarn/colour when a R.S. row is about to be worked. Leave the old colour hanging at the beginning of the row. (You will pick it up again after two rows.) Fold the new yarn over the needle after 'in' so that it makes the first stitch. The first drawing shows how this will look.

Now knit along the row with the new colour to the end. Turn round and work back. Look at the W.S. of the knitting and you will see how the two colours have locked together on that side, but this does not show at the front.

When you have reached the end of the second row, you can now pick up the first colour, drop the new one, and knit two more rows with the first colour. Keep on like this, picking up the other colour after every two rows, and you will see stripes appearing. Don't pull the new colour up too tightly as you begin to knit with it, or the edge will begin to shorten.

The two ends which are left hanging at the bottom of your striped knitting should be darned into the W.S. after the piece is finished.

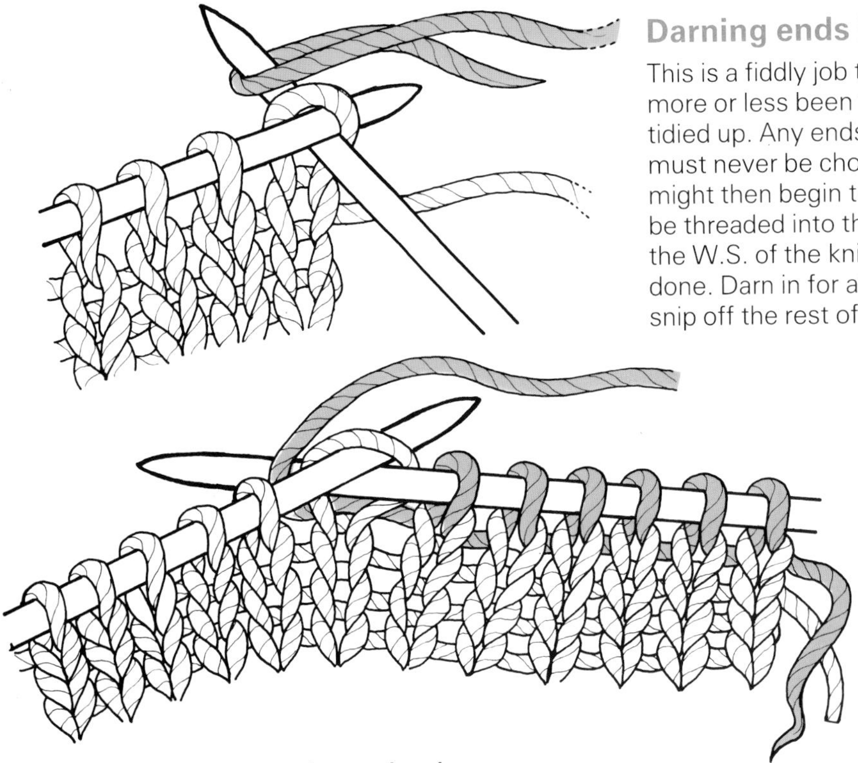

Darning ends in

This is a fiddly job to be done when knitting has more or less been finished and now needs to be tidied up. Any ends which have been left hanging must never be chopped off, because the knitting might then begin to unravel. Instead, they must be threaded into the wool needle and darned into the W.S. of the knitting. Fig 32 shows how this is done. Darn in for about 4cm (1½ins), and then snip off the rest of the yarn.

Fig 31 Knitting in two colours – changing yarns

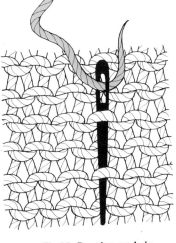

Fig 32 Darning ends in

Three old-fashioned shopkeepers

A table setting for a special person

The growing collection

Mug muffs and coffee-pot muff

An outfit for teddy

Sewing up a knitted edge

The method shown here is known as **the overcast method**: there are other ways, but for the things in this book the overcast method works perfectly well.

Always place two knitted edges with the W.S. up as shown in Fig 33, (or R.S. together) and sew from the W.S. Sometimes the instructions might tell you to sew from the R.S. when it cannot be done any other way.

It is always safest to pin the pieces together first and take the pins out as you sew.

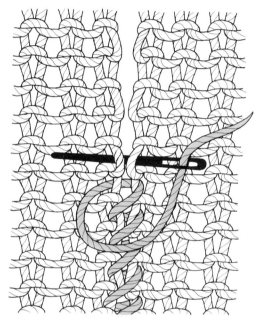

Fig 33 Sewing up a knitted edge

Picking up dropped stitches

Sometimes if you let your stitches stray too near the point of the needle they will drop off. If you find that this happens to you quite a lot, there are two things which might help:

- prevention: keep your stitches a little bit further away from the point and make your fingers hold them in place.
- the cure: have a crochet hook (size 3.50mm) handy as you knit, and rescue the runaway stitch with this. The drawings (Fig 34) show you how to remake both knit and purl stitches with a hook, but you must do this with the points of both needles on each side of the ladder so that you can pop the stitch back on to one of them.

If you find that *all* your stitches have accidently slipped off your needle, they can usually be put back on again as long as the supply yarn is at the end of the row. Always use a *finer* needle to do this so that the stitches will slip on more easily without you having to push. They can then be knitted on to the correct size afterwards.

Picking up a knitted dropped st.

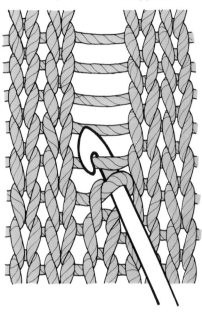

Picking up a purled dropped st.

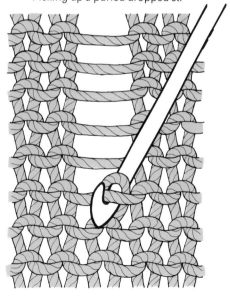

Fig 34 Picking up dropped stitches

Tassels and pompons

These are easy to make from oddments of yarn,
and give an extra finish to even a simple project.
Tassels are just lengths of yarn tied round the top
as shown in the drawing. Darn all ends in neatly.
The drawing on the right of Fig 35 shows how you
might tie it twice for a different effect.

Pompons (Fig 36) are made by wrapping yarn
round two circles of stiff card (1) and then cutting
round the edge when the centre hole is filled (2
and 3). Ease the two pieces of card apart just
enough to get a length of yarn between. Pass the
yarn round the middle between the card circles
and tie it tightly. Remove the cards gently (4). Trim
the pompon with scissors to make a tidy shape,
and use the tie-up ends for sewing on.

Slipping stitches on to a wool needle

Many of the instructions in this book tell you to
slip the last stitches of your knitting on to a
threaded wool needle and gather them together
instead of casting off. This is a neat and quick way
to make the rounded ends of arms, legs and
heads, hats and gloves, and all sorts of other

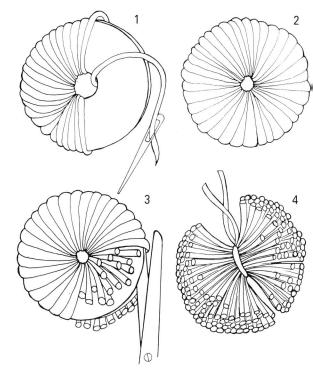

Fig 36 To make a pompon

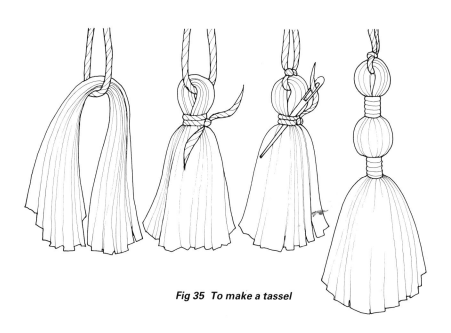

Fig 35 To make a tassel

shaped pieces. Leave plenty of yarn hanging before you cut it off, about 15-20cm (6-8ins) is usually enough, as you may need this to sew up with too. Fig 37 shows how this is done.

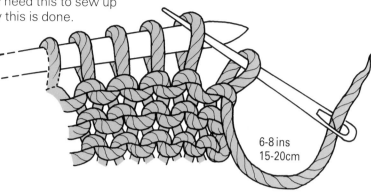

6-8ins
15-20cm

Fig 37 Slipping stitches on to a threaded needle

Running stitch

This tiny stitch is used to gather up the edges of knitting (and other fabrics too) and may be the first one you ever learned to do. The needle goes in and out of the knitting, close to the edge, making the spaces the same length as the top stitches. The dotted lines on the needle in Fig 38 show where it has disappeared on to the other side of the knitting.

L

Fig 38 Running stitch

R

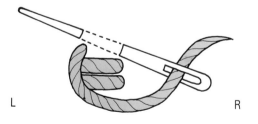

L

R

Fig 39 Satin stitch

Satin stitch

This is an embroidery stitch which is useful for marking in eyes and other small features. Practise making the stitches all the same length and not overlapping each other. Press them down gently with your thumb to make them lie flat. To finish off, bring the point of the needle up well away from the embroidered part where it won't be seen, and snip the yarn close to the fabric.

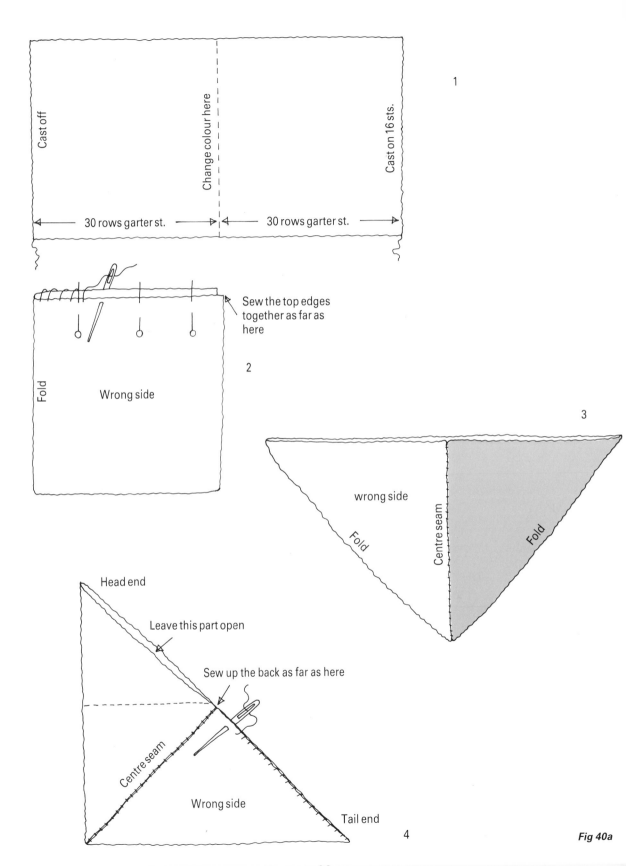

Cast off

Change colour here

Cast on 16 sts.

30 rows garter st.

30 rows garter st.

1

Sew the top edges together as far as here

2

Fold

Wrong side

3

wrong side

Centre seam

Fold

Fold

Head end

Leave this part open

Sew up the back as far as here

Centre seam

Wrong side

Tail end

4

Fig 40a

CHAPTER 4

What Shall I Knit?

Sitting ducks

Every summer, in the village where I live, we have a duck race. Everyone gathers at one of the bridges over the beck (stream) high up where the water enters the village from the hillside. Then along comes a man carrying a huge plastic bag full of yellow plastic ducks, each one with a number round its neck. At a count of five, four, three, two, *one*, the ducks are tipped into the water and prodded into movement by men standing by with long hay-rakes. Then off they go, bobbing along with the current to the bottom end of the village. People race alongside, cheering them on and releasing those which get stuck on the weeds and stones. At the lowest bridge, where the beck leaves the village, a net is strung across to catch them all, and the first one home is placed on the ledge at the top of the arch to watch all the others arrive. His number will be shouted out, and the villager who chose that number will be the winner too, for that year.

These ducks won't be able to swim, but they *can* sit on a high shelf to watch what goes on, like the winner of the duck race.

Materials

To make one duck, you will need two very small balls of D.K. yarn in different colours, a pair of size 4mm needles, scissors, a wool needle, pins and some padding.

Each duck is made from one rectangular piece of knitting in garter stitch, which changes colour half-way.

Method

Cast on 16 sts and knit 30 rows.

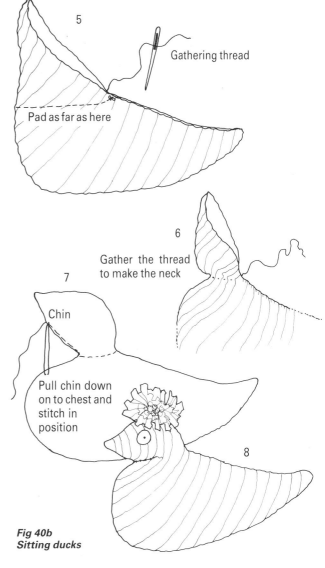

5

Gathering thread

Pad as far as here

6

Gather the thread to make the neck

7

Chin

Pull chin down on to chest and stitch in position

8

Fig 40b
Sitting ducks

Cut the first colour off (leave a longish end) and join in the second colour. Knit 30 more rows and then cast off.

To make up

The drawings (Fig 40) will explain how to make up the duck. Make a small pompon and sew this to the top of the head for extra decoration. Either embroider the eyes or use beads, buttons or sequins, but not if the duck is for a tiny child.

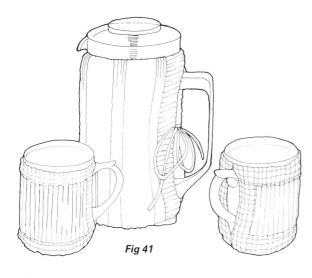

Fig 41

Mug-muff

For those days when people are out-of-doors doing those chilly jobs while their hot drinks get colder and colder on the doorstep or garden wall, this mug-muff is just the thing. If they ask you how they're supposed to drink when there is wool in the way, show them how to fold down the bit where the mouth goes. You could even knit a square mat to go underneath, too, to keep it even warmer!

Materials

For one mug-muff, you will need about 25gms of D.K. yarn, size 4mm needles, scissors and a wool needle.

Measurements

These muffs are designed to fit standard beaker sizes of roughly 9cm (3½ins) tall, and measuring about 22cm (8½ins) round the middle. Your rectangle of knitting may appear to be a little on the small side, but it is meant to fit the mug very snugly.

Method

Cast on 18 sts and work 4 rows in single moss st. Then continue as follows:
Row 5: k1, p1, k1, p1, k10, p1, k1, p1, k1
Row 6: k1, p1, k1, p12, k1, p1, k1
Repeat these 2 rows until the piece measures 20.5cm (8ins).
Finish off with 3 rows of single moss st and cast off in pattern.

To make up

Fold the piece in half and stitch the top corners and then the bottom corners together as shown in the drawing (Fig 41). Darn all ends in and leave the rest of the side open for the handle.

Coffee pot muff

This muff is designed to fit most tall coffee pots, but you can easily check to see whether your knitting is going to be long enough. It is rather like a tea-cosy, but would look especially good in the same colours as your mug-muffs.

Materials

Three mug-muffs and one coffee pot muff take about 100gms of D.K. yarn.

Method

Cast on 54 sts.
Row 1: (k6, p2) 6 times, k6
Row 2: k8, (p6, k2) 4 times, p6, k8
Continue to work these two rows until your knitting measures about 18cm (7¼ins), or for about 50 rows. Measure to see if your knitting will stretch from the bottom of the pot to the top edge. Cast off in pattern.

To make up

Fold the piece in half with the garter stitch edge running from top to bottom. Sew only 2cm (½in) together at the top and bottom edges of the garter stitch to make a large hole for the handle. As this leaves rather a wide gap when fitted on to the coffee pot, a tie should be made at the centre. Make a plaited cord about 60cm (24ins) long, fold it in half and sew the fold to one side of the edge, as shown in the drawing. A tiny loop of yarn at the other side serves to link the two cords and then they can be tied in a bow.

The growing collection

These will brighten any window-sill or table, especially during the winter months when indoor

Fig 42

plants are having a rest. They make good presents for a birthday too and will need no watering or feeding, only a light dusting now and then!

Materials
Use up any small oddments of green D.K. yarns, or use two finer yarns together. Different kinds of green can be used on the same leaf and on the same plant; about 6m (6yds) will be needed for each leaf. Oddments of other colours will be needed for the pompon centres. Each plant will require a small pot measuring 9cm (3½ins) tall and across the top, and a piece of thick card for the base of the plant. Glue, size 4mm needles, scissors, and a wool needle will be needed too.

The leaves
With green yarn, cast on 10 sts and knit one row.
Next row: (tail-end nearest the point of the needle) Increase in the first st, k8, then inc. in the last st
Next row: knit
Repeat these 2 rows until there are 18 sts on the needle, then knit one more row.
Now begin to decrease: k2tog at the beginning of the row, k14, then k2tog at the end
Next row: knit
Repeat these 2 rows (but the k14 will get 2 fewer each time) until you are back to 10 sts on the needle again.
Do not knit an extra row on 10 sts, just cast off. Darn ends in.

If you wish, you can make some smaller leaves by inceasing to only 16 sts before decreasing again.

The flowers
Make small pompons (see page 34) using scraps of brightly-coloured yarns. You will need three or four of these.

To make up
1. Cut a piece of thick card which will just sit comfortably inside the inner rim of the plant-pot. Do not glue it in.
2. Place the card on some newspaper and glue the leaves in position on this as shown in the drawing, allowing some leaves to overlap. Put the not-so-good ones underneath and the better ones on top. Leave a small space in the centre for the flowers.
3. Glue the pompon flowers into the centre, bunching them nicely together and allow it all to dry.
4. Now it can be placed into the top of the plant-pot and given to someone who will appreciate how clever you are.

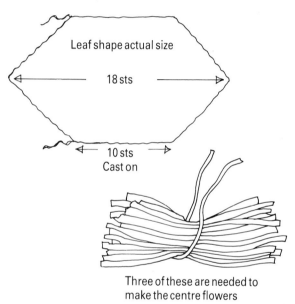

Leaf shape actual size

18 sts

10 sts
Cast on

Three of these are needed to make the centre flowers

Fig 43 The growing collection

Three old-fashioned shopkeepers
These colourful figures are very easy to make; no increases or decreases (except for the pork pie) and almost all in knit stitch. You could make a whole street of shopkeepers like these, standing outside their little shops, perhaps a hat shop, a bread shop or a wool shop!

Materials
You will need small amounts of D.K. yarns and a pair of size 4mm needles, scissors, a wool needle, some thick card and glue, a little padding and some pins. Exact colours are given with the instructions.

How to make the card frame

1. Diagrams 1 and 2 in Fig 44 show you how to cut 3 pieces of thick card, two of them stuck together back to back. One square is for the base. This is the same for all the shopkeepers.
2. Snip the top corners to make a curve for the head, then score across the dotted line and bend this up to make a flat piece.

3. Glue the 2 long pieces together, back to back, then glue the base on (diagram 2).
4. The knitted pieces are fixed around the card frame. Though not *exactly* the same, all are very similar.

The fishmonger
Materials

You will need small amounts of D.K. yarn in dark blue, white, pink, hair-colour, straw-colour for the hat, grey (or any other colours) for the fish, and brown for the tub and base. Also, size 4mm needles, scissors, pins, wool needle and glue, and a very small amount of padding, though this is optional.

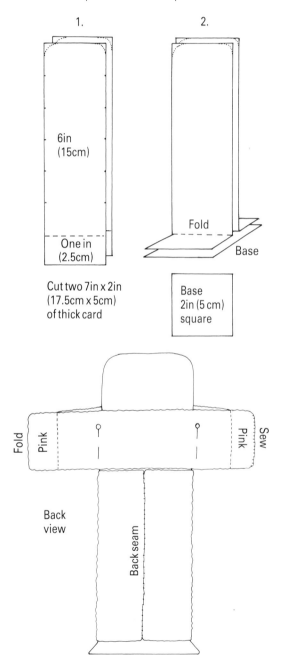

Fig 44 How to make the card frames for the shopkeepers

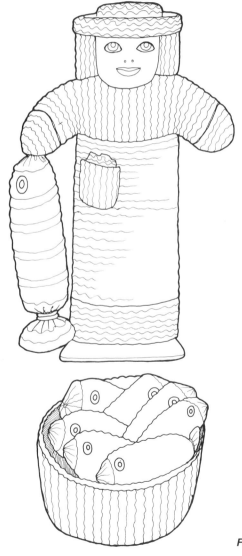

Fig 45

The body

Begin at the lower edge and use the dark blue yarn to cast on 20 sts. Knit 6 rows. Break off the blue yarn. Join in the white yarn and knit 28 rows. Cast off.

Upper body, arms and hands

Using pink yarn, cast on 7 sts and knit 6 rows. Change to white yarn and knit 40 more rows. Change to pink yarn and knit 14 more rows. Change to white yarn and knit 40 more rows. Change to pink yarn and knit 6 more rows. Cast off.
If you look at diagram 3 (Fig 44) you will see how this works.

Face and hair

Using hair-coloured yarn, cast on 6 sts and knit 12 rows.
Change to pink yarn for the face and knit 14 rows. Change back to hair-coloured yarn and knit 12 rows. Cast off.

Base cover (make two pieces the same)

Using base-coloured yarn, cast on 10 sts and knit 8 rows. Cast off.

Pocket

Using white yarn, cast on 6 sts and knit 8 rows. Cast off.

Hat

Using straw-coloured yarn, cast on 8 sts and knit 8 rows. Cast off.

Fish (make about eight of these)

Using grey yarn, cast on 12 sts and knit 30 rows. Do not cast off, but gather the sts on to a wool needle threaded with yarn and draw up tightly. The fish measure roughly 9cms (3½ins) x 3cm (1¼ins).

Tub

This is based on an empty ice-cream tub measuring about 5cm (2ins) deep and about 10cm (4ins) across the top. No knitted base is needed for this.
For the sides, cast on 12 sts and knit a strip long enough to go all the way round the sides. There should be enough extra at the top edge to fold to the inside and cover the top edge of the pot.

To make up

1. Fold the main body piece in half, R.S. together, and sew the two side edges to make a tube.
2. Turn to the R.S. and slip the tube over the card frame with the seam at the back and the blue stripe at the bottom.
3. Fold the body top and arms in half, R.S. together, and pin the two pink hands. Now sew round the two pink hands with pink yarn and turn them R.S. out.
4. Slip this piece over the card figure and pin the

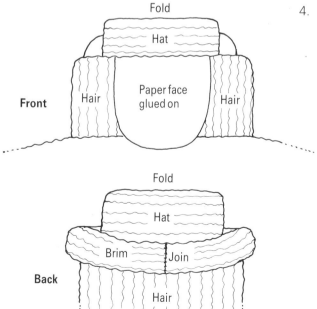

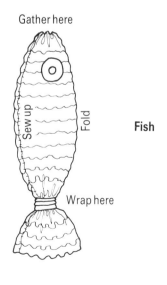

Fig 46 The fishmonger

41

sides of the body as shown in the diagram. Using white yarn, sew the two white pieces together on top of, and underneath, the arms. Now sew this top piece to the main body piece from the R.S. very neatly.

5. If you wish, you can pad between the two pieces *very lightly*.

6. Fold the face and hair piece in half, R.S. together and sew up the two shortest edges. Turn to the R.S. and slide this over the top of the card.

7. Sew neatly all the way round the neck with white yarn.

8. Fold the hat in half and glue this on to the top of the head. Cut out a piece of pink paper for the face and glue this in place. Draw the features on with fibre-tip pens.

9. Now sew up the two short ends of the hat-brim to make a circle, and glue this all the way round the head to sit on top of the hair.

10. Sew the pocket on to the figure, leaving the top open. Can you knit a handkerchief to fit inside the pocket?

11. Glue the two base-covers to the card base, then glue the hem of the skirt in place.

12. To finish off the fish, fold each shape in half along the body, then sew down from nose to tail from the R.S.
Wrap tightly round the tail as shown in the drawing.
Cut 2 tiny paper circles and glue these in place for the eyes.

13. The tub piece should be sewn along the two short edges to make a tube which is then slipped over the carton and stuck in place with glue. Any extra knitting at the top should be folded over to the inside and glued down.

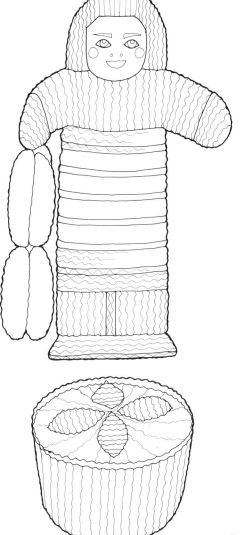

Fig 47

The butcher
Materials
You will need small amounts of D.K. yarn in pink, white, black, grey and dark blue; also hair-coloured yarn. For the pork pie, use brown yarn, and fawn/neutral for the sausages. You will also need a little padding for these, and a plastic carton measuring 7.5cm (3ins) across the base, and 9.5cm (3¾ins) across the top. It should be 6cm (2½ins) deep. If your tub does not agree with these measurements, just make your knitting fit the one you have. Also, size 4mm needles, scissors, a wool needle and glue.

Trousers
Begin at the lower edge and use grey yarn to cast on 4 sts.
Knit 18 rows. Do not break off the grey.
Join in the black yarn and knit 2 rows. Cut off the black.
Pick up the grey and knit 18 rows. Cast off and darn ends in.

Body
Using dark blue yarn, cast on 20 sts and knit 1 row. Do not cut the blue yarn, but join in the white and knit 2 rows.
Now pick up the blue again and knit 2 more rows.

Repeat these last 4 rows of blue and white stripes until you have made six white stripes.
Now knit 2 more blue rows and cast off. Darn ends in.

Upper body, arms and hands
These instructions are exactly the same as those for the fishmonger.

Face and hair
No pink yarn was used for this as the cut-out paper face is stuck on top of the hair-coloured knitting. Using hair-coloured yarn, cast on 8 sts and knit 38 rows. Cast off.

Base
This is the same as for the fishmonger.

Sausages
Using fawn/neutral yarn, cast on about 8 sts and work in either garter or stocking stitch until you have about 25cm (10ins). (The ones seen in the colour picture are made in stocking stitch.) Cast off.

Pork pie
Using brown yarn, cast on 12 sts and knit until the piece is long enough to go right round the tub, then cast off.
To make the top, cast on 50 sts and work in stocking st for 4 rows.
Row 5: (k2tog, k3) 10 times (40 sts)
Row 6: purl
Row 7: (k2tog, k2) 10 times (30 sts)
Row 8: purl
Row 9: (k2tog, k1) 10 times (20 sts)
Row 10: (p2tog) 10 times (10 sts)
Cut the yarn, leaving a long end. Do not cast off but slide the sts on to a threaded wool needle.

To make the leaves, cast on 2 sts and knit them once.
Row 2: inc. into both sts to make 4 sts.
Knit 8 rows on these 4 sts.
Next row: (k2tog) twice and then cast off.
Make 3 more leaves in the same way. Darn all ends in.

To make up
For the body, follow the general instructions set down for the fishmonger, except that the butcher has a narrow strip at the lower edge which represents his trousers (see Fig 47).

1. When you reach the head, sew up the two short sides of the hair-coloured knitting, slide it over the card with the seam at the back and gather the top edge. Sew this tightly together and finish off neatly as shown. Sew the neck edge to the top of the white body.
2. Finish the base, as described for fishmonger.
3. Cut a piece of pink or brown paper for the face, and complete the features with fibre-tip pens. Stick this in place.
4. The diagram shows how to cover the tub with knitting to make the pork pie. Sew the two edges together and then finish off the top. Gather the stitches up as shown, and sew up the gap.
5. Pin the circle on to the top (the widest part) of the knitting and sew all round from the R.S. Darn all ends in, then glue the leaves in place on the top.
6. To make a string of sausages, fold the long strip of knitting lengthways and sew down neatly from the R.S. Gather one end up and stitch this tightly, then place tiny bits of padding into the tube, pushing each bit down with the knob of a knitting needle. At the end of each sausage-shape, wrap yarn round tightly and darn the ends in. Continue towards the top until you have filled all the sausages, and then fold them over to make a neat bunch. Sew these together, and attach them to the butcher's hand with a few stitches.

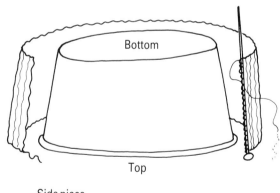

Side piece

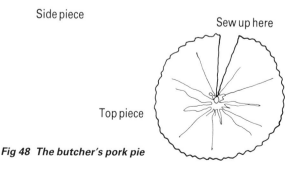

Top piece

Fig 48 The butcher's pork pie

The flower-seller

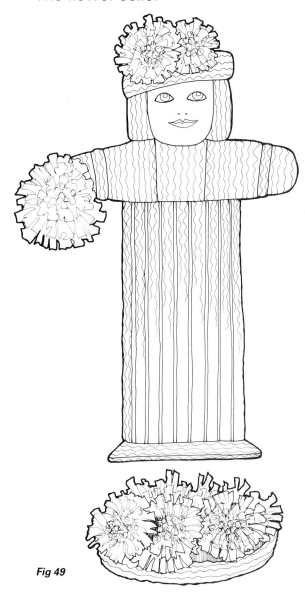

Fig 49

Materials

You will need small amounts of D.K. yarn in pink, white, black, and brown, hair-colour, and some brightly-coloured yarns for the flowers. For the tray, I used the top of the carton which made the Butcher's pork pie. This is about 10cm (3¾ins) across, but a circle of card will do just as well. A little padding may be needed for the upper body, and some glue; also size 4mm needles, scissors, and a wool needle.

The skirt

Using black yarn, cast on 18 sts and knit 2 rows.

Join in the brown yarn and knit 2 rows, leaving the black hanging at the side. Work 2 rows of each colour until you have knitted 40 rows altogether. This piece will go all the way round the card frame with the stripes running downwards. Cast off, and darn in the short ends.

Upper body, arms and hands

These are made as shown in the Fig 50. As each new colour is joined in, cut off the old one, leaving enough to thread into the wool needle so that it can be darned in when you have finished the piece.

Begin with the pink yarn, and cast on 7 sts. Knit 6 rows. Then work as follows:
4 rows of white; 10 rows of black; 12 rows of white; 10 rows of black; 4 rows of white; 14 rows of pink; 4 rows of white; 32 rows of black; 4 rows of white; 6 rows of pink. Cast off, and darn ends in.

Face and hair

Using hair-coloured yarn, cast on 6 sts and knit 12 rows.
Change to face colour and knit 14 rows, then change back to hair-colour and knit 12 more rows. Cast off, and darn the ends in.

Hat

Using black yarn, cast on 30 sts.
Knit one row and then cast off.

Tray of flowers

Cast on about 60 sts and knit 8 rows. Cast off. You will need to make several pompons of brightly-coloured yarns for the flowers. Make as many as you need to squash into the tray, perhaps about six.

To make up

1. Fold the skirt piece with the cast on and cast off edges together. Sew this up and slip it over the card frame.
2. Fold the body top, pinning the colours carefully together from the W.S. and then sew the edges together neatly. Turn to the R.S. and slip this over the card frame above the skirt and sew it in position all round from the R.S.
3. The face and hair piece is made as for the other two figures. Fix in position on the card, and sew on. For the hat, tie the two ends together and glue this circle of knitting round the top of the head at a slight angle. The top (open part)

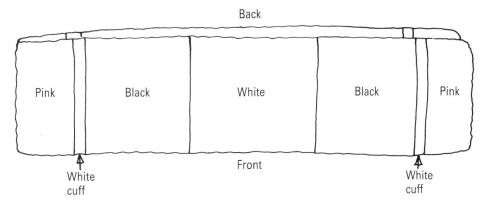

Back

| Pink | Black | White | Black | Pink |

↑ White cuff

Front

↑ White cuff

Fig 50 The flower-seller: upper body, arms and hands

of the head is covered by small pompons of brightly-coloured yarns glued in place.

4. Glue another bunch of pompons into one hand to complete the figure, and make the base as for the other figures.

5. For the flower tray, sew the two short edges of the piece together and run gathering threads round *both* wide edges. Gather these up as shown in Fig 51 and secure the thread. This should cover the edges completely, as the drawing shows. The flowers are glued into the centre.

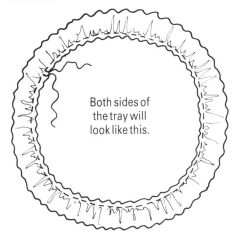

Both sides of the tray will look like this.

Fig 51 The flower-seller: base

Christmas candles

For a pretty table decoration at Christmas (or any other time) make some candles in bright cheerful colours. Plain ones look equally well in a colour to match an all-year-round table setting. Made in one piece, the knitting is fitted over a toilet-roll tube to keep it rigid, and the flame can be made of gold or silver foil (doubled cooking-foil will do quite well).

The separate base is optional.

Stitches
You will need to know garter stitch and stocking stitch, and also how to decrease.

Materials
You will need small amounts of the main colour (A) and the stripe colour (B), in D.K. yarns, and a very small amount of white yarn for each candle. For the white/gold candle, a fine metallic yarn was used double, together with white D.K. used single in between. No base was made for this version.

In addition, you will need size 4mm needles, scissors, pins and wool needle; gold or silver foil for the flame; one toilet-roll tube, 11.5cm (4½ins) x 4cm (1½ins) in diameter; one piece of card for the base, measuring 8cm (3ins) square.

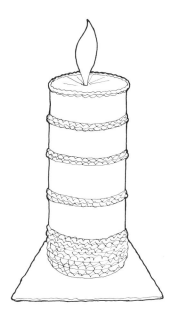

Fig 52

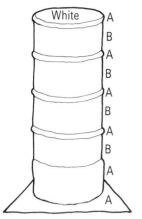

Fig 53 *Christmas candle*

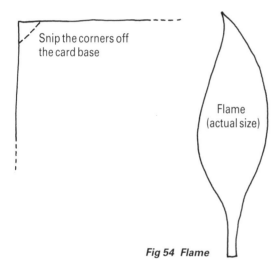

Fig 54 **Flame**

The candle

With colour A, cast on 25 sts (leave a longish end to sew up) and knit 10 rows (garter st).

Change to colour B, but do not cut off A, just leave it hanging.

With B, work 4 rows in stocking stitch, beginning with a knit row.

Next row: pick up A again and knit 2 rows. (This will make the narrow stripe in garter stitch.)

Now repeat these last 6 rows until 4 bands of B and 4 stripes of A have been made, and this will take you to the top edge of the tube.

Now cut off the two yarns (leave ends long enough to darn in) and join in the white yarn. Work 4 rows in stocking stitch.

Next row: (k2tog) 12 times, then k1 (13 sts). Do not cast off, but cut the yarn, leaving enough for sewing up, and slide the 13 sts off on to a threaded wool needle.

The base

Using colour A cast on 15 sts and knit 28 rows. Cast off.

To make up

1. Darn all ends in, except those at the top and bottom.
2. Gather up the stitches at the top of the candle, keeping a tiny hole in the centre. With R.S. together, sew up the white part.
3. From the lower end, thread a wool needle with the cast-on yarn and sew up from the W.S. until the colour changes. Darn the end in.
4. Begin again with colour B and sew up the rest of the piece to the top, matching the narrow stripes across the joins. Turn to the R.S.
5. Slide the cover over the card base (the toilet roll) fitting the last stripe of colour A on to the top rim.
6. Glue around the lower edge and ease the knitting well on to it to cover the card.
7. Snip the corners off the card base (square) and cover it lightly with glue. Place the knitted square over this and ease into position so that the card is quite hidden.
8. Glue all round the lower rim of the candle – the knitting *and* the tube – and position carefully in the centre of the base. Allow to dry.
9. Cut a flame from silver or gold foil (see Fig 54) and place the long end into the hole at the top of the candle.

A table setting for a special person

Whichever special person you choose to make this for, (it might even be yourself), the candle, coasters and napkin rings will make even the simplest meal taste better. Choose any colour to match a favourite tablecloth, mat or tray-cloth. If your cutlery has coloured handles, you could make them to match those too.

Materials

You will need only small amounts of D.K. yarn to make one of the pieces, but if you want to make six, you will need a 50gm ball. You won't need to make more than one candle though! You may need a small amount of metallic yarn for the candle, but only a few metres, and perhaps some beads for the centres of the flowers, but these are optional. You *do* need size 4mm needles, scissors, and a wool needle.

For the candle, see extra materials on page 45.

Candle

The pattern for this is the same as for the Christmas candles on page 45 except that, for this one, only one colour is used and a silver thread has been worked into the garter stitch rows along with the main colour. The eight flowers around the base are like those used on the napkin ring. They are made in the same colours as the candle, including white, and are glued in place.

Coaster

This little mat for a glass or beaker is made on 15 sts in single moss stitch but you can make it in garter stitch if you prefer. The moss stitch version needs 22 rows and the garter stitch one 28 rows. When you have done this, cast off in the same stitch pattern as the knitting, then darn the ends in.

Napkin ring

Cast on 26 sts. Use any stitch you wish, but remember that for single moss stitch you should cast on either 25 or 27 sts and begin every row with a knit stitch. You will need to work about 20 rows. The one in the picture is made in single rib. When you have finished the knitting, sew up the side edges from the W.S., darn all ends in and turn it to the R.S.

Flowers

Cast on 20 sts and work in single rib (or garter stitch) for 4 rows. Do not cast off, but gather the 20 sts on to a wool needle threaded with the remaining yarn and pull tightly to form the centre. Now sew up the two side edges, darn *one* end in, but leave the other end for sewing it on to the napkin ring or candle base.

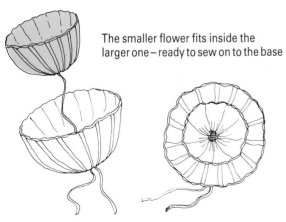

The smaller flower fits inside the larger one – ready to sew on to the base

Fig 55 Flowers at base of candle in place setting

The inside of the flower is made on 12 sts in 2 rows of single rib (or garter st). Gather it up in the same way as the outer part and sew up. Thread the tail-end of yarn down through the centre of the outer part, one inside the other, and sew it in place. Now this can be sewn on to the napkin ring on the opposite side to the seam. If you have a small bead which matches (or a pearl) you could sew this into the centre of the flower before you stitch it in place. Use ordinary sewing cotton for this.

Christmas tree decorations

Sort out your most brightly-coloured oddments of yarn for a set of Christmas tree decorations which will cost almost nothing to make except your time. Take them to school and give them to friends, or decorate the table with them at party-time, one for each guest!

Materials

You will need only small oddments of yarn for these: white for the snowman, coloured bits for his cap and scarf, and the brightest bits you can find for the crackers. If you have some metallic yarn, you could perhaps include this with the D.K. yarns needed for the rest. And, as usual, size 4mm needles, scissors, a wool needle, and padding.

Fig 56

47

Snowman (Fig 56)

Using white yarn, cast on 21 sts and work in either stocking stitch or single moss stitch, or garter stitch if you prefer. Work 16 rows.

Row 17: (k2tog, k1) 6 times, k2tog (13 sts) Work 5 more rows in whatever stitch you are using.

Last row: k2tog to the end of the row, k1 (7 sts) Cast off.

To make the hat, use bright coloured yarn and cast on 16 sts. Knit 3 rows (g.st). Do not cast off, but thread the stitches on to a wool needle threaded with left-over yarn. Draw up tightly and sew up the two side edges to make a cup shape. Darn the ends in.

To make the scarf, use the same yarn and cast on 30 sts and knit 2 rows. Cast off and darn the ends in.

To make up

1. Turn the snowman shape to the W.S. and sew up the two side edges, leaving the bottom open but closing the top.
2. With white yarn in the wool needle, run a gathering stitch round Row 17 (where you began to decrease) – this is the neck. Before you draw up the thread, place a tiny bit of padding into the head space, then gather the neck gently and fasten off securely. Now pad the body to make a smooth round shape and sew up the bottom edges with white yarn.
3. Embroider two eyes and a nose and some buttons on to your snowman, then stitch (or glue) his hat on at an angle.
4. Fold the scarf around his neck and stitch this in place with matching yarn. Thread some white or black cotton through the top of his hat and tie this in a large loop ready for hanging on the tree.

Christmas cracker

Cast on 20 sts and work 26 rows in stocking stitch. Cast off. The R.S. can be either the smooth or the rough side. Fold the piece edge to edge, and sew it up from the R.S., leaving the ends open. Wrap a length of yarn tightly round the cracker a short distance from each end to make a neck. Fasten the ends off very securely. Thread black or white sewing cotton into one end to make a loop for hanging.

A bow for your pet

Your pet deserves a colourful decoration too, so why not make a smart bow to tie on to his collar or harness? You may even decide to wear it yourself instead!

Materials

You will need very small amounts of deep green and some red for the centre tie, all in D.K. thickness. Also 2 metres of white yarn for the plait, size 4mm needles, scissors, a wool needle, and pins.

Method

For the main part of the bow, use the deep green and cast on 10 sts. Knit 70 rows in garter stitch to make a piece measuring 5 x 17.5 (2ins x 7ins). Cast off.

For the centre tie, use the red yarn and cast on 12 sts. Knit 8 rows and then cast off.

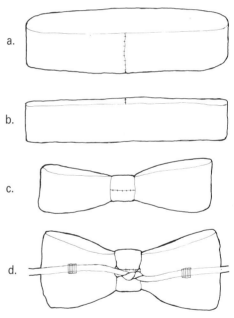

Fig 57 A bow for your pet

To make up

1. Fold the main piece in half and sew up the two short sides to make a tube. (See Fig 57.) Darn the ends in (a).
2. Fold this piece flat with the seam at the centre back (b), and wrap the red piece round the middle. Pin the edges at the back and sew them together (c).
3. Now make a plait for the tie from three lengths of yarn, one red, one green and one white,

Two jolly clowns

Sitting ducks

A wardrobe of clothes

Christmas candles

Christmas tree decorations

Snowman and Santa Claus

each 2 metres long. Fold these lengths in half and hook the fold over someone's finger or a door handle.
4. Divide the six strands into three pairs of different colours, and plait them from top to bottom.
5. Tie an overhand knot at each end and trim with scissors.
6. Thread this plait through the red section on the bow and tie halfway along the plait (d).
7. Make a few firm stitches into the plait and the back of the bow to keep it lying in the right direction when it is tied on. Now it is ready to be given to your pet on Christmas morning.

The snowman (Fig 58)

Though we may not be able to make a real one outside, this comfortable little man will stay with us without melting even in a warm room. He is the same size as the Santa Claus, 20cm (7¾ins) tall, and they are great friends!

Materials

You will need about 25gms of white D.K. yarn and small amounts of coloured yarns for the hat and scarf. Oddments of dark yarns are needed for the face and buttons. Also, size 4mm needles, scissors, a wool needle, pins, some padding and a piece of thick card for the base.

Fig 58

Body and head

Although the snowman in the picture is made in double moss stitch to imitate the texture of snow, any other stitch can be used instead on the same number of stitches.

Using white yarn, cast on 40 sts and work 42 rows.
Row 43: (k2, k2tog) 10 times (30 sts). This is where the head begins
Row 44: purl
Work 10 more rows in stocking stitch for the head.
Next row: k2tog across all sts to the end of the row and then cut off the yarn about 15cm (6ins) from the last stitch. Thread this on to a wool needle and slide the sts on to the yarn.

Hat

Using coloured yarn, cast on 30 sts.
Rows 1, 2 and 4: knit
Rows 3 and 5: purl
Row 6: k2tog across all sts to make 15
Row 7: purl
Do not cast off, but finish off in the same way as for the head.

Scarf

There are two methods for you to choose from:
● Using coloured yarn, cast on 8 sts and knit until the scarf measures about 25cm (10ins) long. Cast off. Darn ends in.
● Using coloured yarn, cast on 60 sts and knit 6 rows. Cast off and darn ends in.
(The scarf in the picture is made by the second method.)

To make up

1. Fold the main body piece inside out with the edges together, and pin these in place. Gather the top of the head tightly and sew down all the way to the base.
2. Thread the wool needle with white yarn and make a running stitch all the way round the neck. Pad the head gently and then gather the thread up to make a neck. Fasten off securely.
3. Pad the body to make a nice rounded shape like the one in the picture.
4. Use the diagram (see the diagrams for Santa Claus) to make a card base.
5. Thread the wool needle with white yarn again and make a running stitch round the lower edge of the body, into the cast-on edge..
6. Slip the piece of card inside the knitting just

to cover the padding and then draw up the thread to enclose it. Fasten off securely.

7. Embroider the eyes, nose and mouth with dark coloured thread.
8. The hat: gather the top with the thread and use this to sew up the edges. Make a small pompon from scraps of yarn and stitch or glue this to the hat. Darn all ends in.
9. Place the hat on the head at an angle and stitch or glue it in place.
10. Darn the ends of the scarf in, wrap it round the snowman's neck and tie it on.
11. Embroider buttons down the front where they will not be hidden by the scarf.

Santa Claus

This cheerful Santa with his sack of goodies will be a favourite with young and older people too. He is not at all difficult to make, even though there are many parts to him. And the pattern on the sack might be your first ever attempt at working from a chart. It won't matter if it goes slightly wrong; no one will notice, least of all Santa!

Materials

You will need a 50gm ball of red D.K. yarn, small amounts of white, pink, brown, light brown (for the sack) and grey. Size 4mm needles, scissors, wool needle, pins, padding and a small piece of thick card for the base.

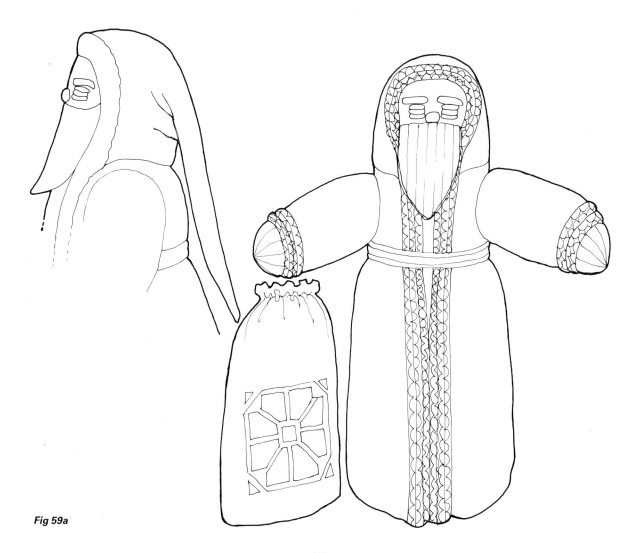

Fig 59a

Measurements

The figure is 20cm (7¾ins) tall and measures 24cm (9½ins) round his widest part.

Tension

5 sts and 7 rows over stocking stitch will make 2.5cm square (1 square inch).

Body and head (made in one piece)

Using red yarn, cast on 40 sts and work 2 rows in single rib. Now change to stocking stitch and work 28 rows, beginning with a knit row.

Row 29: (k3, k2tog) 7 times, k5 (33 sts)
Row 30: purl
Row 31: change to moss st. Begin every row with a knit st and work 11 rows.
Row 32: (W.S.) (k2, k2tog) 8 times, k1 (25 sts). Cut the red yarn.
Row 43: Join in the pink yarn and begin with a knit row. Work in ss for 10 rows.
Row 53: (k2tog) to the last st, k1 (13 sts). Do not cast off, but cut the yarn about 15cms (6ins) away from the last st and thread this on to a wool needle. Gather the last 13 sts on to the yarn and leave this aside for the moment.

Arms and hands (make two the same)

Using red yarn, cast on 15 sts and work 10 rows in moss st.
Leave about 15cm (6ins) of yarn hanging and cut the rest off.
Join in the white yarn and knit 4 rows (g.st). Cut off the white yarn and join in the pink.
With pink yarn, (k1, k2tog) to the end of the row (10 sts).
Next row: purl.
Now work in ss for 2 more rows. Do not cast off, but gather the stitches up in the same way as before. Darn all ends in.

Front bands and hood

Using white yarn, cast on 94 sts. (This sounds like a lot, but don't be put off, you will only need to knit one row.)
Row 1: knit
Row 2: cast off 32 sts, knit to the end of the row
Row 3: cast off 32 sts, knit to the end of the row, leaving 30 sts in the middle of the needle for the hood
Row 4: (R.S.) Cut off the white yarn and join in the red. Knit.
Row 5: purl
Row 6: k2tog, k12, k2tog, k12, k2tog

Row 7: purl
Row 8: k2tog, k11, k2tog, k10, k2tog
Row 9: purl
Row 10: k2tog, k9, k2tog, k9, k2tog
Rows 11, 12, 13, 14 and 15: work in ss without shaping
Row 16: k2tog, knit to the last 2sts, k2tog
Row 17: purl
Row 18: knit
Row 19: purl
Repeat rows 16, 17, 18 and 19 until only 13 sts are left. (There should be 28 red rows at this stage.) Now continue to k2tog at *both ends* of every knit row until there are only 5 sts left. Slide these sts on to a length of yarn as you did for the head and arms.

The beard

Using white yarn, cast on 10 sts and work in single rib for 4 rows.
Row 5: k2tog, (k1, p1) 3 times, k2tog (8 sts)
Row 6: (p1, k1) 4 times
Row 7: k2tog, (p1, k1) twice, k2tog
Row 8: (k1, p1) 3 times
Row 9: k2tog, k1, p1, k2tog (4 sts)
Row 10: (p1, k1) twice
Row 11: (k2tog) twice and cast off

The belt

Using dark brown yarn, cast on 60 sts. Cast off without knitting any rows. If you prefer, you can make a twisted cord, a plait or a crochet chain instead.

The sack

Using light brown yarn, cast on 30 sts. Without the charted white pattern on the sides, all you need to do is to work in ss for 26 rows and then cast off. But if you want to make the pattern, work 4 rows of ss to begin, and join in the white on the 5th row.

You will see that there are 30 squares across from one black line to the other: these are your 30 stitches. You will begin the pattern in white yarn with the R.S. facing you (a knit row) and this is numbered Row 1. All the purl rows begin at the other end and are numbered with even numbers. This should help you to remember where you are. The white squares are the red stitches and the crosses are white stitches.

To make up

The diagrams should give you a fairly clear idea of

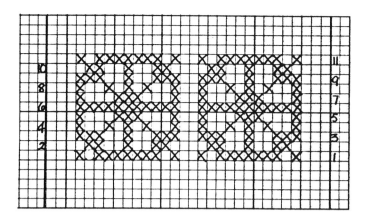

Fig 59b Pattern on Santa's sack

how the pieces are put together. Begin by darning all unwanted ends in neatly.

The body and head

1. Fold the piece with R.S. together and pin the edges. Sew all the way up to the top of the head, taking care to match the red and pink in the right places. The seam now goes at the centre back.
2. Place a small piece of padding into the head end, thread a wool needle with red yarn and make a running stitch round the neck, beginning at the back seam. Draw this up *very* slightly and tie the two ends together.
3. Place more padding into the top half of the body where the moss stitch is, and then into the lower body. The base should be left open until the front bands have been sewn on (Fig 60a).

The arms and hands

4. Sew up the side edges of the arms, changing the colour of the thread with the knitting. Pad the shapes gently.
5. Pin the arms to the body so that they are angled slightly forward at an equal distance from the back seam. Now sew these in position all the way round the openings (Fig 60b).

The face

6. Stitch the beard across its top edge halfway across the face, leaving the pointed end free. Embroider two large grey or blue eyes above this, then the white eyebrows and finally, the pink nose. See the stitch diagrams on page 50. Check that all ends have been darned in.

Fig 60 Santa Claus

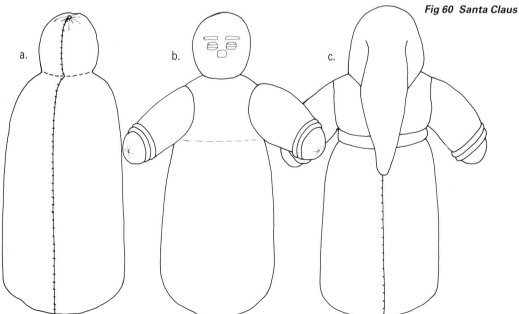

a. b. c.

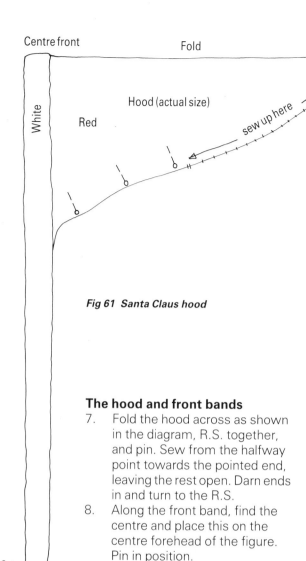

Centre front   Fold

White

Red

Hood (actual size)

sew up here

Fig 61 Santa Claus hood

The hood and front bands

7. Fold the hood across as shown in the diagram, R.S. together, and pin. Sew from the halfway point towards the pointed end, leaving the rest open. Darn ends in and turn to the R.S.
8. Along the front band, find the centre and place this on the centre forehead of the figure. Pin in position.
9. Place the end of each band at the centre hem of the figure and pin these in place. Pin the bands all the way up to the neck, underneath the beard.
10. With white yarn, sew the hood in position beginning at the R.S. underneath the beard, continue round the head drawing the hood closely on to the face as you go, then down the L.H. front band. Now sew up the R.H. front band back to where you began. Note: sew along the *middle* of the band using a back stitch.
11. The lower edge of the hood can now be pinned into place on the shoulders (c). Pull the open sides of the hood well down on to the shoulders and back and stitch in place, matching the centre seam to the centre back seam of the figure.

To finish

12. Tie the belt around the waist and position the knot at the back, tucking the ends in out of the way.
13. At the base, run a gathering thread round the edge of the knitting. Do not fasten off. Cut a piece of card in the shape shown in the diagram and put this just inside the knitting at the base. Gather up the thread gently and pull the knitting just over the edge of the card. Fasten off securely and darn ends in.
14. Fold the sack piece in half, inside out, and pin the two sides together. Sew along the bottom and sides, then turn to the R.S. Pad the sack to make it look full and then gather the top edge with a length of yarn and tie the ends in a knot. Make a loop to sling over Santa's shoulder.

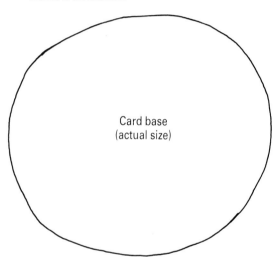

Card base
(actual size)

Fig 62 Snowman and Santa Claus base

Two jolly clowns

The two jolly clowns are both made from the same pattern, but the colours are changed over. Only two pieces are needed: the body, head and hat are knitted all-in-one and the collar is made separately. They are padded to give them a soft cuddly shape, and each has a base of card to make it stand flat. In the pattern, the two colours are called A and B; A being the colour which is used to cast on the main body piece, and B being the colour of the collar and hat.

They have different collars in the colour picture: the blue one in double rib and the yellow one in garter stitch. Choose whichever you prefer.

Fig 63

Stitches
You will need to know how to knit and purl for stocking st., how to decrease and how to rib – if you choose!

Measurements
From the base to the top of the hat – 20.5cm (8ins).

Materials
You will need small balls of D.K. yarn in blues and yellows. These need not all be the same; different oddments can be used up together. A small amount of white D.K. for the face is necessary, together with tiny bits of red and brown for the eyes and mouth. Also, size 4mm needles, scissors, pins and a wool needle, card for the base and some padding and glue.

The body, head and hat
With yarn A (see the notes above) cast on 30 sts and knit 2 rows.
Next row: purl
Now work 4 rows in ss, beginning with a knit row. Do not cut off yarn A. Join in yarn B. In B, knit 4 rows (this makes a garter stitch stripe). Leave yarn B hanging, and work 6 rows in ss with yarn A, beginning with a knit row. Now continue like this:
B: 4 rows knit; **A:** 4 rows ss; **B:** 4 rows knit; **A:** 2 rows ss; **B:** 4 rows knit; **A:** 4 rows ss. This is the end of the body, now begin the head.

Leave about 10cm (4in) of A and B yarns, and cut the rest off. Join in the white yarn and work 2 rows in ss beginning with a knit row. Now decrease for the neck as follows: (k2tog, k1) 10 times (20 sts). Now work 7 rows in ss beginning with a purl row. This is the face, now begin the hat.

Leave about 10cm (4ins) of white yarn, and cut off the rest. Join in yarn A and knit 2 rows. Cut off A and join in B. With B, work 2 rows in ss beginning with a knit row. To shape the hat to a point, begin to decrease as follows:
Next row: (k2tog, k2) 5 times (15 sts)
Now work 3 rows in ss beginning with a purl row.
Next row: (k2tog, k1) 5 times (10 sts)
Now work 3 rows in ss as above.
Next row: (k2tog, k1) 3 times (7 sts)
Work 3 more rows in ss as above.
Next row: (k2tog) 3 times k1 (4 sts)
Next row: p4
Last row: (k2tog) twice, then cast off.

The collar
For the yellow garter stitch collar, cast on 50 sts and knit 8 rows.
Row 9: k2tog across all sts to make 25. Cut the yarn, leaving a long end, and thread these last sts on to it.
For the blue ribbed collar, cast on 50 sts and work 8 rows in double rib.
Row 7: k2tog, p2tog across all sts to make 25. Complete as for the yellow callar.

To make up

Body, head and hat
1. Fold the large piece down the centre with the two side edges pinned together, and use the

leftover yarn at the top of the hat to sew downwards. When you reach the white/head part, use white yarn, and change colour again for the body. Skip over the bands of different colours on the way down, then thread your wool needle with the second colour and close all the small gaps which were left open.

2. Using white yarn, make a running stitch all the way round the neck where the first white row begins. Do not gather.

3. Place a little padding inside the hat and arrange it with knitting needle to form a point. Pad the head gently. Gather the neck thread and finish off securely.

4. Now pad the rest of the body to make a smooth shape as seen in the pictures.

Base

5. Cut a disc of firm card measuring 5cm (2in) across, and glue this on top of the padding just inside the base. Pull the knitting just over the edge of the card and glue the knitting in place. The first two rows of knitting should fit on to the card edge.

Collar

6. Slip the sewn-up collar over the clown's head, gather the thread and finish off securely. Use the same thread to stitch the collar to the neck all the way round.

7. Make two very small pompons from yarn A and sew one to the top of the hat and the other to the front of the body.

8. Embroider the face with red straight stitches for the nose and mouth and a large brown cross for each eye.

A wardrobe of clothes (Fig 64)

These well-known figures need quite a lot of clothes to keep them looking smart and warm. As they are almost all the same size, they will be able to wear each others' clothes without you having to do much to change the sizes. The only one which will need changing is the trousers, which will be just a little too long for the younger girl, so the length of the legs will have to be shortened by a few rows. You may also have to shorten the sleeves of the green jacket, but that only means knitting fewer rows. None of the patterns have any increases or decreases, they are *all* made of rectangular pieces.

Measurements

The figures stand 30cm (12ins) and 27cm (10½ins) tall. Other measurements are given with the garment instructions.

Fig 64

Stitches

To make all these garments, you will need to know how to knit and purl to make garter stitch and stocking stitch, but don't worry if you don't know how to purl as all of them can be made in plain knitting if you prefer. Single and double rib are also used.

Tension

5 sts and 8 rows over stocking stitch on size 4mm needles will make 2.5cm square (one square inch).

5½ sts and 10 rows over garter stitch on size 4mm needles will make 2.5cm square (one square inch).

Materials

Only small amounts of D.K. yarn are needed for these garments; about 25gms will make the short jacket, skirt, hat and bootees. The man's coat and trousers take a 50gm ball of yarn (together) and the sweaters need about 20gms each, but there will be enough left over to make extra bootees, hats, scarves and belts. Also needed: size 4mm needles, scissors, wool needle, row-counter, tape measure, pins, and a note-pad and pencil for noting any points to watch as you go along. A stitch-holder is needed for the hooded jacket.

Fig 65 Short garter stitch skirt

Short garter stitch skirt (cream) (Fig 65)

Using cream yarn, cast on 30 sts and knit 40 rows. Cast off.

To make up

Fold the piece in half and sew the two side edges together; this is the centre of the back. Thread a cord or length of yarn through the waist and tie to keep the skirt in place, or use elastic.

Longer ribbed skirt (mauve)

Using mauve yarn, cast on 48 sts and work in double rib until the piece is 10cm (4in) long. Then cast off.

To make up

Fold the piece in half and sew the two side edges together; this is the centre of the back. Finish off in the same way as for the short garter stitch skirt.

Jumper with sleeves (orange) (Fig 66a,b)

The back and front are both the same: make one of each. Using orange yarn, cast on 16 sts and work in single rib for 6 rows. Now change to stocking stitch and work 12 rows, beginning with a knit row (18 rows altogether). Next row, work in single rib, then cast off in rib.

Sleeves (make two the same)

Cast on 20 sts and work in single rib for 2 rows. Now work 10 more rows in ss. Cast off.

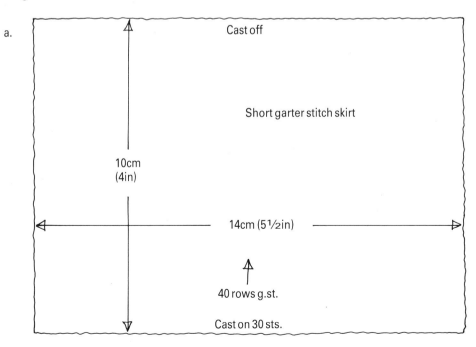

a.

Cast off

Short garter stitch skirt

10cm
(4in)

14cm (5½in)

40 rows g.st.

Cast on 30 sts.

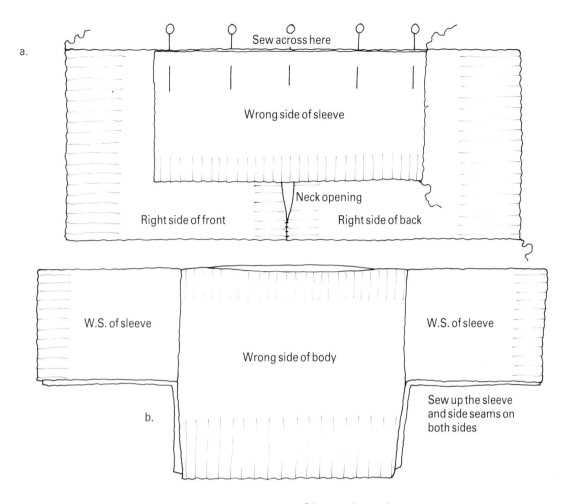

a.

Sew across here

Wrong side of sleeve

Neck opening

Right side of front   Right side of back

W.S. of sleeve   W.S. of sleeve

Wrong side of body

Sew up the sleeve
and side seams on
both sides

b.

Fig 66a,b Jumper with sleeves

To make up

1. With the R.S. on the inside, place the two body pieces together and pin the shoulders. The ribbing at the lower edge will be the waist. With the same coloured yarn, make just 2 or 3 sts at each side of the neck opening, leaving plenty of room for the head.
2. Lay these two pieces flat out and lay one of the sleeve pieces on top with the R.S. together. Pin them together (Fig 66a) then sew along the edge to fix the sleeve to the body.
3. When this has been sewn on, fasten off and sew the other sleeve to the other side in the same way.
4. Now fold the whole piece across, inside out (Fig 66b), and sew round the side and sleeve edges.
5. Turn the jumper to the R.S. and darn all ends in neatly.

Sleeveless jumper (mauve) (Fig 67)

The instructions for this are the same as for the orange jumper except that it has no sleeves. Make

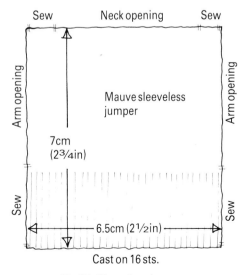

Sew   Neck opening   Sew

Arm opening

Arm opening

Mauve sleeveless
jumper

7cm
(2¾in)

Sew

Sew

6.5cm (2½in)

Cast on 16 sts.

Fig 67 Sleeveless jumper

it up in the same order as the other, shoulders first, then side seams, but only sew where the ribbing is. The rest is left open to give plenty of room for the arms. Finish off in the same way.

Man's white jumper with sleeves

The back and front are both the same; make one of each. Cast on 18 sts and work 3 rows in single rib.
Change to stocking stitch and work 28 more rows.
Next row: purl. Cast off.

Sleeves (make two the same)
Cast on 16 sts and work 2 rows in single rib.
Change to stocking stitch and work 16 more rows.
Cast off.

To make up
The instructions are the same as for the orange jumper with sleeves on page 56. Be sure to leave plenty of room for the head.

Trousers (make two pieces the same)

Cast on 18 sts and work 2 knit rows, then one purl row.
Now change to ss (begin with a k row) and work 47 more rows.
Cast off.

To make up
1. From the cast off-edge, count down 14 rows and mark this point with a pin. Do this on both pieces.
2. Place the two pieces, R.S. together, and pin the top *side* edges as far down as the pin markers (Fig 68a).
3. Sew down as far as the pins on both sides.
4. Fold the pieces across the other way so that this seam is now at the centre (Fig 68b). Now sew up the inside leg edges on each side, all the way down to the bottom edges.
5. Turn the trousers to the R.S.
6. Make a plaited, twisted or crocheted cord and thread this through the top to tie round the waist.

Short striped jacket in garter stitch

Make it in stripes, or all in one colour, whichever you prefer. This is made in five pieces: a back, two sides and two sleeves.

Back
Cast on 18 sts and knit 48 rows.
Cast off.

Fronts (make two pieces in the same way)
Cast on 8 sts and knit 48 rows.
Cast off.

a

14 rows

Sew the two side edges together as far as the pins

Stop here   Stop here

Trousers (wrong side)

b

Fold the pieces across the other way so that this seam is now at the centre

Now sew up the inside leg seams on each side

(wrong side)

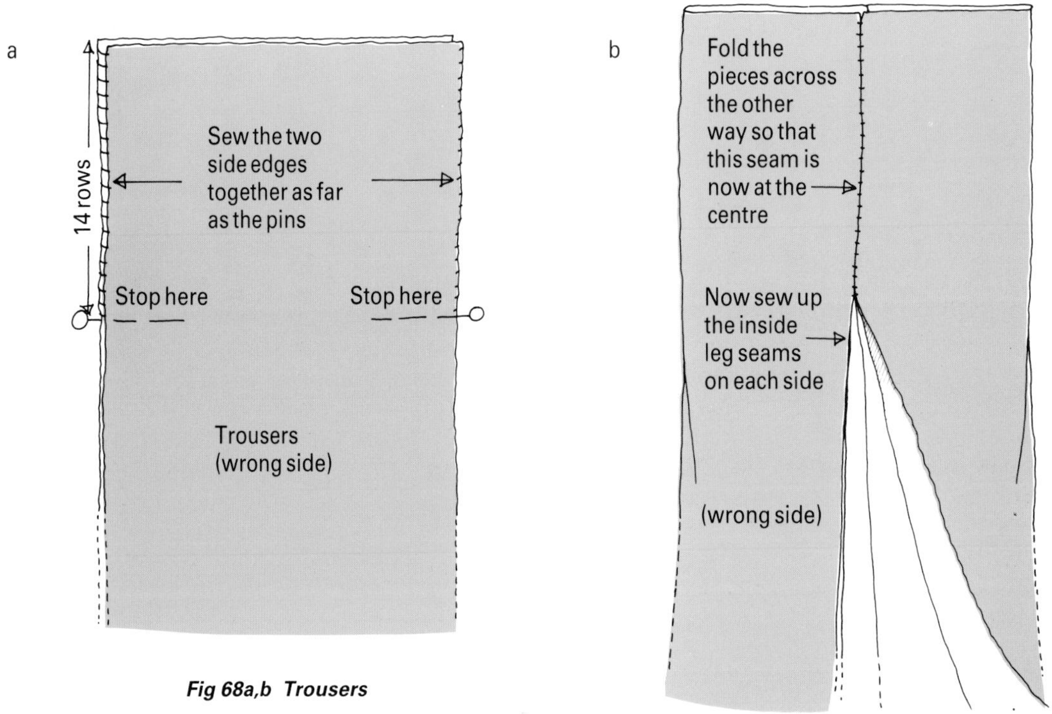

Fig 68a,b Trousers

Sleeves (make two pieces in the same way)
Cast on 18 sts and knit 18 rows.
Cast off.

To make up

Basically, the instructions are the same as for the jumpers. Fig 69 shows the layout of the pieces. Begin with the shoulder seams, and finish by darning all ends in.

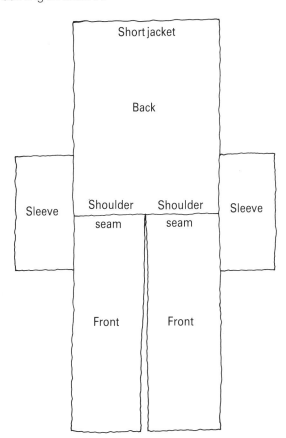

Fig 69 Short striped jacket in garter stitch

Long hooded jacket (to match the trousers)
This jacket is made in a mixture of garter stitch and stocking stitch, and looks good over trousers or a short skirt. The hood is made all-in-one-piece with the front panels and back, so stitch-holders will be required to keep the stitches safely until you are ready to put them all together.

Back

Cast on 22 sts and knit 2 rows. Then purl one row. Now work in ss for about 40 rows, or until the piece measures 15cm (5¾in) from the beginning, ending with a purl row.

Next row: cast off 5 sts and knit to the end of the row.
Next row: cast off 5 sts purlwise and purl to the end of the row.
Now leave the remaining 12 sts on a stitch-holder (or a spare needle).

Right front panel

Cast on 14 sts and knit 2 rows.
Row 3: p10, k4
Row 4: k14
Repeat the last 2 rows until the piece measures the same as the back as far as the shoulders, then knit one more row.
Next row: cast off 5 sts purlwise, and purl to the last 4 sts, k4.
Leave about 25cm (10in) of yarn hanging, and cut off the rest. Leave these 9 sts on a stitch-holder, or spare needle.

Left front panel

Cast on 14 sts and knit 2 rows.
Row 3: k4, p10
Row 4: k14
Repeat the last two rows until the piece measures the same as the back and right front panel as far as the shoulders.
Next row: cast off 5 sts and knit to the end of the row.
Purl one more row, but do not break off the yarn. Now you have three pieces of knitting waiting to have the hood knitted on.

To pick up the stitches for the hood

1. Begin with the right front panel and knit the 9 sts from the stitch-holder (in your left hand) on to an empty needle (in your right hand), tying on more yarn if you need to.
2. Now knit the 12 sts from the back piece on to the same needle as the right front panel so that the two are now side by side on one needle.
3. Take the stitch-holder holding the 9 sts of the left front panel and knit these too on to the same needle, but use the attached ball of yarn to do this.

Now you have all three pieces on one needle, and your next row will be a purl row across all 30 sts.

[**Note**: if you do not want to make a hood, make a collar instead by knitting about 8 rows and then casting off.]

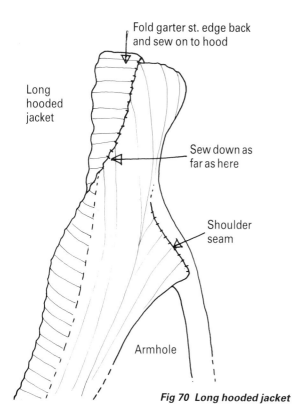

Fold garter st. edge back and sew on to hood

Long hooded jacket

Sew down as far as here

Shoulder seam

Armhole

Fig 70 Long hooded jacket

Hood
On the 30 sts (the purl row); k4, p22, k4
Next row: knit
Repeat these two rows 7 more times (16 rows altogether).
Cast off.

Sleeves (make two in the same way)
Cast on 18 sts and knit 2 rows
Next row: purl
Work 22 rows of ss and then cast off.

To make up (Fig 70)
Do the same with this jacket as for the other garments, joining the shoulders first, then the sleeves and then the side and underarm seams all in one. The diagram will help you to see how this will look (Fig 70). Turn the cuff back on each sleeve to fit your model. Fold across the top of the hood and complete as shown in the drawing.

Young lady's hat
Use the same yarn and needles as for the jacket, and cast on 20 sts. Knit 14 rows but do not cast off. Gather all the stitches on to a length of yarn threaded on to a wool needle, draw up tightly and sew up the sides. Darn all ends in.

Bootees
Cast on 6 sts and knit 10 rows. Do not cast off but gather up in the same way as for the hat and sew up the sides. Make two of these.

Man's brown boots
Using brown yarn, cast on 14 sts and work in ss for 14 rows. Leaving plenty of yarn for sewing-up, cut off the rest, thread on to a wool needle and gather the stitches on to this. From the W.S., sew up the two side edges and darn ends in. Turn to the R.S. and slide this on to the foot so that the seam lies along the *outside edge* of the leg. Make another in the same way.

An outfit for teddy
Is it time your teddy had some new clothes? The one in our picture is now over twenty years old and so we thought it was time he had a new tee-shirt, jacket and shorts.

As he is quite a large teddy (48cm [19in] tall and 38cm [15in] around his waist) we thought it best to use a thicker chunky yarn for his jacket and shorts. So if your teddy is a bit smaller than this, you could use D.K. yarn and size 4mm needles and the result will be a smaller version. Exact measurements of all the clothes are given under the separate headings: you can change them any way you wish to fit your own teddy's measurements.

Materials
A tweedy chunky yarn was used for the jacket and shorts. Two 50gm balls are needed for the jacket alone. Jacket and shorts together take three 50gm balls, but there will be enough left over to make a pair of bootees for winter, or a woolly hat. Size 5mm needles are used with this yarn.

The tee-shirt takes one 50gm ball of white D.K. yarn, knitted on size 4mm needles, and you will also need three tiny white buttons. And also, stitch-holder, scissors, wool needle, tape measure (just to check measurements), and pins.

Tension
With chunky yarn on size 5mm needles, 4 sts and 6 rows to 2.5cm square (one square inch).
With D.K. yarn on size 4mm needles, 5 sts and 8 rows to 2.5cm square (one square inch).

Stitches
Garter stitch, stocking stitch, double rib. Decrease.

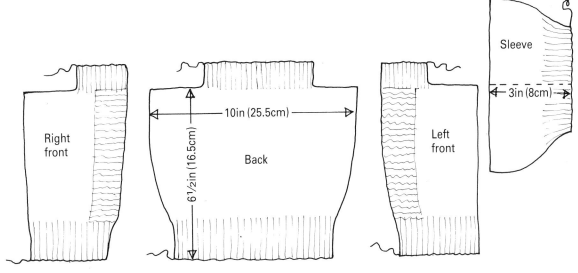

Fig 71 Teddy's jacket

The jacket

This has long sleeves with ribbed cuffs, collar and welt, and a garter stitch border down the front. It has no fastenings, as bears have trouble undoing buttons. He manages to get his tee-shirt over his head without unfastening it!

Measurements: across the back 25.5cm (10in); length of sleeve 8cm (3in); length of body from shoulder 15.5cm (6¼in).

Back

Cast on 32 sts and work in double rib for 8 rows.
Row 9: (inc. in next st, k3) 8 times (40 sts)
Row 10: purl
Now continue in ss until the piece measures 15.5cm (6in) from the cast-on edge, that is, about 34 rows.
Next row: (R.S. facing) Cast off 10 sts. Knit to the end of the row
Next row: Cast off 10 sts purlwise. Purl to the end of the row (20 sts). Now work in double rib for 6 rows.
Cast off in rib.

Right front panel (teddy's right, not yours)

Cast on 16 sts and work in double rib for 8 rows.
Row 9: (inc. in next st, k3) 4 times (20 sts)
Row 10: p14, k6
Row 11: k20
Repeat the last two rows until 35 rows have been worked, counting from the cast-on edge.
Next row: (W.S. facing) Cast off 10 sts purlwise; p3, k6

Now work in double rib for 6 rows, then cast off in pattern.

Left front panel (teddy's left)

Cast on 16 sts and work in double rib for 8 rows.
Row 9: (inc. in next st, k3) 4 times (20 sts)
Row 10: k6, p14
Row 11: k20
Repeat the last 2 rows until 34 rows have been worked, counting from the cast-on edge.
Next row: (R.S. facing) Cast off 10 sts, k to the end of the row.
Now work in double rib for 6 rows, then cast off in pattern.

Sleeves

These are usually one of the largest pieces on human garments but teddies have short arms so these are very much smaller and quite quick to make. Make two exactly the same.

Cast on 32 sts and work 8 rows in ss.
Row 9: (k2, k2tog) 8 times (24 sts)
Row 10: purl
Now change to double rib and work 6 rows.
Cast off in pattern.

Making up

1. With R.S.s together, pin the right front shoulder to the right back shoulder, and sew the two edges together. Now do the same with the left side.
2. Lay the knitting out flat, R.S. upwards. Take one sleeve and mark the centre of the cast-on edge with a pin.

3. Now place this centre-marker on the shoulder seam, edges together and R.S.s together. Pin the two pieces in position and sew them together.
4. Do the same with the other sleeve on the opposite side.
5. Fold the jacket over, inside out, and pin the sleeve edges and the side edges together, then sew along the sleeve and the side edge all at the same time. Do the same at the other side. Darn all ends in securely.

The Shorts

These are made in two pieces, both the same. They are sewn together down the centre front and centre back.

Method

Cast on 40 sts and knit 6 rows (g.st).
Row 7: purl
Row 8: knit
Repeat these 2 rows until there are 29 rows altogether, ending on a purl row, from the cast on edge. This will measure about 13cm (5in).
Next row: (k3, k2tog) 8 times (32 sts).
Next row: work in double rib, and continue in this st for 5 more rows. Cast off in pattern. Make another piece in the same way.

Making up

1. With R.S. together, take one piece and fold it in half as shown in the diagram. Pin the lower (g.st) edge and stitch this part for 2.5cm (1in) as far as the change from g.st to ss. as shown in Fig 72b. Do the same with the other piece.
2. Lay both legs side by side and match up the front and back edges. Pin these together from the W.S. all the way round from front to back, then sew up.
3. Turn to the R.S. If Teddy needs help to keep them up, you can thread the top with a plaited, twisted or crocheted cord.

The tee-shirt

Front

Using white D.K. yarn and size 4mm needles, cast on 46 sts and knit 5 rows.
Row 6: purl
Continue in ss for 7.5cm (3in) (i.e. 23 rows from the cast-on edge). Begin the armholes and neck-opening as follows:
Row 24: (W.S. facing) k6, p14, k6, p14, k6

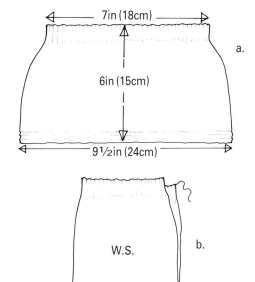

Fig 72a,b Teddy's shorts

Row 25: knit
Row 26: k6, p14; now slip the 26 sts from the L.H. needle on to the stitch-holder and leave them there while you work one side. Turn the knitting so that you are now ready to begin a knit row.

You now need to make a little flap which will tuck underneath the other side of the neck-opening to hold the buttons. It's quite simple – at the beginning of the new knit row (20 sts) you must cast on 6 more new stitches. Put your R.H. needle into the first stitch and begin to cast on as you did at the start. When you have made 6 new sts, check to see if you have 26.
Now knit across all 26 sts.
Next row: k6, p14, k6
Repeat the last two rows until there are 13 *purl-ridges* on the sleeve edge, counting from the end of a purl row, i.e. with the needle pointing towards the centre.

Now shape the neck as follows:
Change to g.st and k8 rows.
Next row: cast off 13 sts, k to the end of the row.
Knit on the remaining 13 sts for 7 more rows, then cast off. One side is now complete, and we have to go back to the sts on the holder to do the other side.

When you undo the stitch-holder, do it carefully

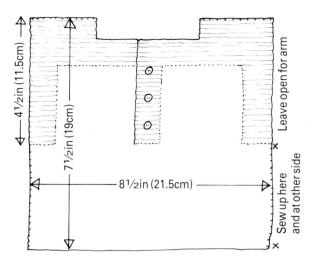

Fig 73 Teddy's tee-shirt

(Diagram labels: 4½in (11.5cm); 7½in (19cm); 8½in (21.5cm); Leave open for arm; Sew up here and at other side)

and have your empty knitting needle ready to take the stitches as they slip off the point. Slide all 26 on to the needle and have your yarn ready to join in. For the first stitch, loop the yarn over, just like joining in a new colour. Your needle will now be pointing towards the centre, so the first row will be a purl row, but first, there is a band of 6 knit stitches which will lie over the top of the other one. This band will have buttonholes on it.

First row: k6, p14, k6
Next row: knit

Repeat these two rows once more, then the first row again.

Now we need to make the first buttonhole, and this is done by making a k2tog and then a 'pretend stitch' by laying the yarn over the needle. This makes a hole. Follow the instructions.

First buttonhole row: (R.S. facing) k22, k2tog, bring the yarn to the front as if you were going to purl, but *knit* the next two stitches and let the yarn lie on top of the needle, pretending to be a stitch. This is called a *yarn-forward*, or *y.fwd.*
Second buttonhole row: k6, p14, k6.
You will have to knit into the yarn-forward even though it is a bit floppy and sits rather oddly on the needle. But don't let it escape – you need it! Can you see the tiny hole for the button now?

Work 6 more rows straight between each buttonhole, then work two more buttonhole rows again. Make three buttonholes altogether with 6 rows between each. When you have made three of them, you should have 13 purl-ridges on the sleeve edge also, and the needle should be pointing towards the side, ready for the next knit

row. This is where we change to garter st. Knit 7 rows.

Next row: (W.S. facing) Cast off 13 sts and k to the end of the row.
Knit straight for 7 more rows and then cast off.

The back

Cast on 46 sts and knit 5 rows.
Row 6: purl
Continue in ss for 23 rows from the cast-on edge.
Begin the armhole as follows:
Row 24: (W.S. facing) k6, p34, k6
Row 25: knit
Repeat these last two rows until there are 13 purl-ridges on the R.S. at the armhole edges (26 rows).
Knit one more row.
Next row: Knit across all 46 sts.
Work 5 more rows, ending with a R.S. row.
Next row: (W.S.) k33 and slide the last 13 sts on to a stitch-holder. Turn and cast off 20 sts.
Knit 12 sts from the L.H. needle (13 altogether) and knit 6 rows on these 13 sts. Cast off.

Slide the 13 sts from the stitch-holder on to one needle and join in the yarn again to knit across all these sts. One row.
Now, with R.S. facing, knit 5 more rows, then cast off.

Making up
1. Place the two pieces, R.S.s together and pin the shoulders. Sew these together and darn the ends in.
2. Tuck the 6 cast-on sts on the front opening *behind* the buttonhole panel and stitch the bottom edge in place across the 6 garter sts.
3. Pin the two sides together below the garter st sleeve-openings. Sew these on both sides, leaving the garter st parts open.
4. Sew on three small buttons which will pass through the holes.

Index